From the
Trash Pile
to the
Treasure Chest

Creating a Godly Legacy

Leah Adams

CROSSBOOKS
PUBLISHING

CrossBooks™
A Division of LifeWay
1663 Liberty Drive
Bloomington, IN 47403
www.crossbooks.com
Phone: 1-866-879-0502

First published by CrossBooks 9/24/2010

ISBN: 978-1-6150-7333-7 (sc)

Library of Congress Control Number: 2010913141

Printed in the United States of America

This book is printed on acid-free paper.

Contents

Week 1—Creating a Godly Legacy   1

   • Day 1—Why Is a Godly Legacy Important?   2

   • Day 2—Setting an Example   5

   • Day 3—A "Hinge" Moment   8

   • Day 4—The Sign of Scarlet   10

   • Day 5—Back to Basics   12

Week 2—Legacy Building Block 1: Faith   15

   • Day 1—What Is Faith?   16

   • Day 2—A Faith Tested   19

   • Day 3—He Will Never Forsake You   21

   • Day 4—What's His Name?   24

   • Day 5—Is God Who He Says He Is?   28

Week 3—Promise-Keeping   31

   • Day 1—Promises, Promises   32

   • Day 2 – God's Promise to Abraham   35

   • Day 3—God's Promise to David   38

   • Day 4—God's Promises about Jesus   41

   • Day 5—What about Me?   43

Week 4—When Character Was King   47

- Day 1—A 5:22 Picture of Character   48
- Day 2—The Gossip Girls   52
- Day 3—May the Words of My Mouth …   55
- Day 4—Liar, Liar, Pants on Fire   57
- Day 5—Standing By Your Word   60

Week 5—The Pursuit of Holiness   63

- Day 1—What Do I Know of Holy?   64
- Day 2—Goats and Treaties   68
- Day 3 – Dress for Success   71
- Day 4—Disobedience and Regrets   74
- Day 5—Shun the Appearance of Evil   78

Week 6 –Trash Pile to Treasure Chest—Legacies to Consider   83

- Day 1—I Did It My Way   84
- Day 2—Channy's Story   88
- Day 3—Finally, I Know Him!   93
- Day 4—A Legacy Check-Up   100
- Day 5—Legacy Check-up: Part Two   104

Introduction

The first speaking engagement God allowed me was on Valentine's Day weekend at Macedonia Baptist Church in Hiawassee, Georgia. The event was the church's annual widow's brunch, at which time the church honored those church ladies who had lost their husbands to death. As I prayed and asked the Lord to give me a topic and Scripture that would speak to that particular audience, I sensed that He wanted me to focus on the topic of "legacy." Most of the ladies who were being honored were older and had seen quite a few years come and go. There would certainly be a wealth of wisdom and some godly legacies among them.

My focal Scripture for that event was 2 Timothy 1:3–5, in which the apostle Paul reminded young Timothy of the great legacy of faith that belonged to Timothy through his mother, Eunice, and his grandmother, Lois. This seemed like a fitting topic and passage of Scripture on which to focus for a group of ladies who were still active and spiritually seeking, even if it was without their life partners. My fifteen-minute message was well received, and I went home feeling that I had pleased the Lord with what I had done.

Little did I know that this topic of legacy would become what author Margaret Feinberg calls a "sacred echo" in my life. Repeatedly over the course of the next two years, the topic of legacy would surface. Time and again, the Lord made it evident that this message about creating a godly legacy would be the message that I would offer to one ladies' group after another. Each time I have taught this message, the Lord has given me new information and Scriptures to add to it. In fact, this message has become my hallmark message, for it is based on the things that God has taught me over the course of forty-six years of doing this thing called life.

We live in a world that is all about the here and now rather than the there and then. Our mottos are "if it feels good, do it" and "it's all about me." The simple fact is that it is *not* all about us. I see generations of young girls and women who have never been taught the importance of a noble character or the value of "shunning the very appearance of evil." Our young women today are learning about character and holiness from mainstream fashion and lifestyle magazines. To our shame, Christian women are sitting comfortably in soft pews in white-washed churches and allowing the world to teach its values to our young women. We, the body and bride of Christ, should be the ones teaching our young women how to be women of faith who believe in the one true God; women who exhibit noble character and holiness before God. This is our calling in this generation.

When God made it clear to me that I was to put the legacy message into a Bible study format, my heart was thrilled and a bit apprehensive. My legacy has not always been a treasure chest legacy. For many years, the trash pile was where my legacy originated, because I refused to factor God into my life's equation. Oh, I was saved and a Christian, but I was not living like one. Much of what you will find in this study I learned on God's field trips. I'm not one who seems able to learn in the classroom. No, not me; I have to take the field trip and learn the hard way. Let me assure you that God is not hesitant to take you on a field trip if that is the only way you will learn. My hope is that my field trip experiences will teach you the importance of living a life that leaves a godly legacy for those who come behind you—because, really, when all is said and done and you are walking this earth no more, what others remember about you will be your legacy.

I'm thrilled that you are considering joining me in this legacy-building endeavor. I must warn you: at times the journey will be uncomfortable when we examine our faith, character, and holiness. God's desire is to peel away everything of the world from our lives so that we will shine brightly for Him. Ask Him to help you stay the course during these six weeks of study. Purpose in your heart to do whatever it takes to leave a treasure chest legacy.

During this study, you will have five days of homework to complete each week. Do your best to complete all of it, as this work is crucial to understanding the broad scope of your legacy. I hope you are doing this study with a group of women who love to chat and discuss and share. Your experience will be greatly enriched by times of group discussion about what you have studied. However, if you are doing the study on your own, that is okay. I believe the Holy Spirit will engage in much heart-to-heart discussion with you about the material. Whatever your circumstance, I am thrilled you are taking this journey with me, and I look forward to hearing from you about your experience with *From the Trash Pile to the Treasure Chest: Creating a Godly Legacy*. Know that I am praying for you and esteem you greatly for your efforts in Bible study.

Captured by His Grace,

Leah

Acknowledgments

When I consider my life and the paths I have walked, I have to smile at how gracious the Lord has been to me. He took a woman whose legacy was plucked straight off the trash pile of tabloid magazines and gave me a hunger and thirst for Him and His Word. Nothing created by humankind could have made the impact on my heart and life that the Holy Word of God has produced. In short, the time that I have spent over the past decade in the Word and in sweet fellowship with Jesus has turned my legacy into one that is more befitting a treasure chest. So my deepest gratitude goes to the One who gave His life for me; the One who loves me unconditionally and completely. Thank you, sweet Jesus, for taking a prodigal and using her to point other precious hearts to You. I pray that I will always be as faithful to You as You have been to me. To the King, who is eternal, immortal, and invisible: I love You, Jesus!

My parents, Wayne and Barbara Colwell, gave me wonderful examples of love, dedication, perseverance, humility, and selflessness to follow. Thank you, Daddy and Mother, for your love and support and for the legacy you have left me.

Two of my extended family members encouraged me to begin writing in 2003. Depending on how you feel about this Bible study when you complete it, you can either thank or fuss at my uncle, Jack Parker and my cousin, Carol Addington-Pate. Their words of encouragement in those early days were what gave me the confidence to explore the art of writing. Thank you both for investing in me.

The ladies in my Tuesday morning small group Bible study have been incredibly generous in their encouragement and time. Their willingness to work through a draft of this study and give me honest feedback helped tremendously. God blessed me incredibly with this group of friends and Bible study partners. Thank you, my friends. You are precious gifts from God.

Finally, to my husband, Greg, who is also my dentist. I married so far above me. Thank you for your patience with the seemingly endless hours of writing. God has used you in so many ways to turn my legacy from one that belonged in the trash pile into one fit for a treasure chest. Your character, personal integrity, and wisdom offer me countless opportunities to admire you deeply. Thank you for loving me and sticking with me through the good times and the bad. I love you.

Week 1—Creating a Godly Legacy

Welcome! Or as we say in the South, "Hey!" This week, you and I will begin to think about the topic of legacy, and along the way we will ponder why in the world we should even care about our legacies. I will share part of my own family legacy with you, and we will peer into a family in antiquity and see that no matter how far down we fall, it is never too late to begin building a godly legacy for the generations that come behind us.

In truth, whether we realize it or not, we are all building our legacies each and every day. Those who come behind us will remember us for the things we did and said, as well as the things that we failed to do or say. The responsibility for leaving a wonderful legacy lies with each of us. I cannot create your legacy, nor can you create mine. When I walk my final mile on this earth, I want to know that I have not left a trash pile legacy, but rather that I have left a treasure chest legacy for those who come behind me. My guess would be that you do too. What we leave for the generations that come behind us really does matter.

Leaving a godly legacy is what Psalm 145:4 is all about. "One generation will commend your works to another; they will tell of your mighty acts." When our lives overflow with the love, grace, and mercy of Jesus, we are commending His works and telling of His mighty acts to others. That, my friends, is a wonderful legacy to leave to those who come behind us. Join me as we begin our journey toward a treasure chest legacy.

Week 1 Goals:

- Understand the importance of leaving a godly legacy.

- Identify the key event that must take place if we are to leave a godly legacy.

Day 1—Why Is a Godly Legacy Important?

As I begin to write, I ponder on the people who will one day sit with this Bible study before them, and I wonder a few things about them—about you. I wonder what brings you to this Bible study. Why are you interested in a Bible study about creating a godly legacy? What season of life are you in? Are you a young mom who has suddenly realized that she is setting an example for those little ones who cling to her legs? Perhaps you are a single who desires to stand out above the crowd of "everyone is doing it." You might be a grandparent who recognizes that time is flying by and you have fewer and fewer days with which to make a significant difference in your family. Maybe you are someone whose heart has been so battered and bruised by circumstances or the words or actions of others that you cannot imagine ever being at the point where your life makes a difference for the cause of Christ. Perhaps you are someone like me who spent a significant part of their life pitching their tent in a pit of sin and rebellion, pushing away the Jesus who gave His all for you. Do you sense that the Lord is bringing you to the point of understanding that it is crucial for the next part of your life to be dedicated to something other than yourself?

Whatever brings you to this study, I welcome you, and I invite you to jump in wholeheartedly, holding nothing back. Allow the fresh wind of the Holy Spirit to bring you to a place of complete submission to the work of Christ in your life. In order for you to leave the legacy that Christ desires, you must be willing to give Him free reign of your heart and mind. You and I must be obedient to Romans 12:1, where Paul encourages us to offer our bodies as living sacrifices. If there is junk that needs to be cleaned out, *cooperate* with Him. It is only by truly offering Him all of yourself—mind and body—to work with that your legacy will be the masterpiece that He knows is possible.

I want to ask you to pause right now and allow me the honor of praying for you as you begin this journey toward creating a godly legacy for those who come behind you.

"Dear Jesus, You left us the perfect example of how to create a godly legacy. I pray for this precious one who sits before You with an open Bible, open workbook, and open heart. I ask You to bless her for taking the first step toward a godly legacy. Create in her a willingness to allow the Holy Spirit to sweep through her heart, exposing anything that separates her from You—anything that needs to be cleansed. Please give my friend fresh ears and a fresh heart to hear You speaking as we take this journey toward building a godly legacy together. I pray she will be diligent in her study of Your Word, knowing that it is through Your Word that our faith is increased and our lives are changed. Please make yourself real to her as she seeks to live a life that is pleasing to You—a life that will impact the succeeding generations for the cause of Christ. Help us, Lord, to build a godly legacy for those who come behind us. In Your matchless name, the name of Jesus, I ask this prayer. Amen."

This topic of legacy was seared into my spirit when I participated in Lisa Whelchel's Bible study, entitled *This Is My Story: Creating a Scrapbook Legacy of Faith.* As I created my own personal scrapbook detailing my life story, I realized that I, indeed, had a story. Mine was not the most exciting story—and in fact, some of it was pretty ugly—but it was *my* story to tell.

In this Bible study, you will hear pieces and parts of my story. You will meet my parents, grandparents, and other family members. You will get to know my friends and see how they are building their own legacies. I will be honest about some very difficult times in my life where I made poor choices that impacted my legacy. Yet I will also share with you times that I made good and right choices. All of this is part of the legacy I leave for the generations that come behind me. God doesn't wait until we are pushing up daisies in some graveyard to begin using our legacies to impact future generations. He is using parts and pieces of my story today to impact those around me. He will do that with your story, too. So let's get to it.

Were you aware that the Bible speaks to this issue of our legacy? In 2 Timothy 1:3–5, Paul points toward a legacy of faith. Read 2 Timothy 1:3–5 and answer the following questions:

- To whom was Paul writing/speaking?

- Who passed the legacy of faith down to Timothy?

- In 1 Timothy 1:2 and 2 Timothy 1:2, how did Paul refer to Timothy?

Let's take a moment and remind ourselves a bit about Timothy, his family, and their relationship with Paul as we begin to think about building a legacy. The book of 2 Timothy was written by Paul in approximately AD 66 or 67 and was Paul's final letter in his earthly ministry.

It is obvious that Paul felt much like a father to young Timothy, who in all likelihood would have been no older than his early thirties at the time 2 Timothy was written. There are at least two reasons why Paul would have felt a fatherly affection for Timothy.

First, it is likely that Paul led Timothy to a saving faith in Christ, since over and over in the Scriptures, Paul called Timothy his "son in the Lord." The second reason Paul seemed to be a father figure in Timothy's life is one that is not so obvious.

- Record everything you learn about Timothy's family and the part that their religion played in their lives in Acts 16:1 and 2 Timothy 1:5.

In Acts, we learn that Timothy's mother and grandmother were women of faith, and that is once again confirmed in 2 Timothy 1:5. What is noticeably absent is any mention of the faith of Timothy's father. We are told that Timothy's father was Greek, but most scholars assume that he was not a believer in Jesus. Only the faith of Timothy's grandmother and mother are mentioned as being of significance, so perhaps Paul functioned as the spiritual leader for Timothy—the spiritual father figure that Timothy did not have, either because his father was not a believer or because his father died when Timothy was young.

Whatever the reason, Paul made sure that young Timothy understood the importance of building a godly legacy, and Paul underscored that fact by setting an example himself, as well as highlighting the legacy of faith that belonged to Timothy because of his mother and grandmother.

I would like for us to go to one additional passage of Scripture that I believe Paul might have had in mind as he reminded young Timothy of his legacy of faith. In Psalm 78, we find the psalmist, Asaph, encouraging the Israelites to consider their legacies and the importance of passing knowledge of God from one generation to the next.

- Read Psalm 78:1–7. Verse 7 tells us, in no uncertain terms, the reason for leaving a godly legacy. Using your own words, write what Asaph said to the Israelites.

Every generation has unique God-stories. You have your own unique stories of God-encounters that are part of your legacy. Do not bottle these stories up and let them die within you. These are stories that need to be shared with others so they, too, can be encouraged to remain faithful to God and His commands.

What will you leave for the generations that come behind you? It is my prayer that you will leave incredible stories of the faithfulness of God in your life. Today, my friend, let's begin shaping our legacies.

Meditation Moment: Think about the people who have gone before you and left legacies for you. It might be a material legacy, a spiritual legacy, a legacy of hard work, or a legacy of faithfulness to a cause. Describe in a few sentences the legacy someone has left to you, and then voice a prayer of thanksgiving to God for that person and the influence they have had in your life.

Day 2—Setting an Example

Yesterday we looked at the legacy that Timothy had been given by his mother, grandmother, and his spiritual father, the apostle Paul. Today, let's delve deeper into the meaning of the word *legacy*.

The word legacy is never used in the Word of God, yet the concept permeates the Bible. The Encarta Dictionary defines the word *legacy* as "money or property that is left to somebody in a will; something that is handed down or remains from a previous generation or time."[1] Synonyms for legacy include *inheritance, birthright, bequest,* and *heritage.* The words *inheritance, birthright,* and *bequest* cause one to think of money or property being handed down. In contrast the words 'legacy' or 'heritage' bring to mind things handed down that lie in the realm of the spiritual or moral.

Allow me, if you will, to share part of the legacy that I call my own. On April 7, 1936, Wayne Edward Colwell was born to Frank and Eula Colwell in Blairsville, GA. He would be their only child and would be watched over and protected fiercely, especially by his mother. Only moments old, he struggled to live, and at one point was wrapped in a blanket and "laid out for dead," as the old-timers

used to say. It was only when one of his aunts noticed the blanket moving that the family realized he was very much alive. A few months later, he would struggle with a serious case of pneumonia that threatened his life. Yet by God's grace, he overcame that as well.

In June of 1952, Wayne became very sick and was diagnosed with polio. He spent weeks at Grady Memorial Hospital in Atlanta, where he endured excruciating spinal taps and other medical procedures necessary to diagnose and treat this horrendous disease. Ultimately, polio would leave him unable to walk without the aid of a full leg brace and crutches. His parents could only see him once a week while he was at Grady, and this contributed all the more to his mother's overprotective spirit. After several weeks at Grady, he was moved to Warm Springs Rehabilitation Center, where he spent several months learning to live with the residual effects of polio. He was told that he would never walk again and would be forced to spend the rest of his life confined to a wheelchair.

After coming home, Eula would have waited on Wayne hand and foot had she been allowed. However, Wayne had learned a measure of independence at Warm Springs, and he was determined that he would not allow his handicap to disable him. He finished high school, attended Young Harris College, and obtained his broker's license to sell real estate. In his real estate business, he often needed to walk the properties that he was buying or selling, and with the aid of the full leg brace to keep his atrophied leg straight and crutches to keep him upright, he did just that. He achieved great success in the real estate business and also served a term as the sole commissioner of the county where he lived.

Not only was he successful in business, but he was a wonderful father to his two daughters and husband to his wife, Bobbie. His life evidenced his love for Jesus, and he volunteered untold hours mowing the grass for First Baptist Church in Blairsville. His passion was to see young people encouraged in their walk with Christ, and he gave generously to the youth program at First Baptist.

On the day of his memorial service, over 800 people stood in line for several hours to pay their respects to Wayne. His family heard story after story of how he had helped people in the community in a very quiet way.

"He paid my mortgage payment to keep me from losing my home."

"Wayne came by the appliance store, purchased a washer and dryer, and told me to deliver them to so-and-so. He told me never to tell who paid for them."

Over and over, the stories were shared. These stories evidenced a life well lived—a life that left a legacy of hard work, integrity, perseverance, wisdom, and love for his Lord and his fellow man.

Wayne was my daddy, and over the years, I watched him function as well as any man who had two good legs. He provided very well for our family, when he could have easily given up and depended on charity or the government to support us. He was a respected business man whom people trusted because of his honesty and integrity. He worked hard and persevered in spite of his handicap. God gave to him wisdom, keen insight, and vision, and he used them to be the man God desired for him to be. It was from my daddy's example that I learned about perseverance, hard work, and integrity.

Let's take a look at a few people in the Bible who set examples for others. Look up the following passages and record who set an example for others to follow and what example did they set:

- Genesis 2:2–3

- Genesis 12:1–4

- Joshua 7:1–26

- 2 Samuel 9:1–7

- Psalm 51:1–6

- Jonah 1:1–3

- Luke 22:39–42

- John 13:3–17

- Acts 5:1–10

People are watching us each and every day of our lives. As we go about our days, we are—either consciously or unconsciously—setting an example for others. In the things that we do and say, we are writing our story on the lives that surround us. Have you considered the story you are writing on the lives of those surrounding you?

MEDITATION MOMENT: Make a list of the people with whom who you consistently interact. After praying and asking the Lord to give you insight, note what the Lord tells you about the example you are setting for each of those people.

Day 3—A "Hinge" Moment

Welcome back to our examination of the legacies of people in the Bible. It is important for us to remember, as we examine biblical legacies, that those we are studying were not so different than you and me. They were normal people living everyday lives. They were women and men, wives and husbands, business people, homemakers, grandparents, sisters, and brothers. They were people who experienced all the same emotions that we feel: love, impatience, irritability, joy, exasperation, and so much else. Their lives were not the lives of comic book superheroes who magically transform from ordinary to extraordinary with only the snap of a finger or the blink of an eye. They were common people met by an awesome God who transformed them into uncommon saints. That, dear friend, is what God desires to do with my life and with your life.

Join me as we visit with one of these uncommon saints today.

Turn to Joshua 2 and read the entire chapter, then answer the following questions:

- To which city did Joshua send the spies?

- Who did they meet there?

- What was Rahab's occupation?

- What kind of legacy was Rahab creating for her family up to this time?

I find it very intriguing that Rahab, who was a prostitute, would have a heart tendered toward the Lord at the very moment the spies from the Israelite army came into the city. Coincidence? I think not.

- What does Joshua 2:9–11 tell us about the perception of the Israelites and their God by the people of Canaan and the city of Jericho?

It is obvious that God's Spirit had gone ahead of the Israelites and caused a fear of them to fall on the people of Canaan. Jericho was a well-fortified city and would have presented a huge obstacle to the Israelites as they entered Canaan. Archaeological evidence exists that confirms the city walls of Jericho consisted of double walls built about fifteen feet apart. The king and people of Jericho were trusting in their man-made wall of protection against outside enemies. Rahab, on the other hand, had come to the conclusion that her people were in big trouble and that she needed to do something different if she were to avoid complete destruction.

It appears that no sooner did the spies enter the house of Rahab and tell her of their mission, than she agreed to hide them, knowing that it wouldn't be long before they were brought to the attention of the king. Joshua 2 tells us that apparently the spies did a poor job at keeping their mission secret. Almost as soon as Rahab pulled the flax over them, the king's henchmen were pounding on her door!

It is at this point in Rahab's story that we find the hinge. What do I mean by the hinge? The "hinge" is what I would like to call that point in the life of a person when they realize they need to do something different than what they have been doing in order to have a different—and hopefully better—outcome.

Rahab is at a hinge moment in her life. She has heard the stories of the God of Israel and how He has shown Himself as mighty in their behalf. Rahab has likely been one of those spirited women who was just fine on her own and didn't really need anyone else to take care of her. In truth, she probably had not had anyone who cared enough to take care of her for many years.

Yet when the hinge moment comes and she must choose between trusting in other people or trusting in the God of Israel, Rahab's heart is prepared to swing in a new direction and trust God. Suddenly, Rahab is on a new road, going in a different direction. This is the road of trust in an unseen—yet very evident—God who will do amazing things in and through her, if she will let Him.

Let's come back tomorrow and visit with Rahab a bit more. For now, take a moment and ponder our daily meditation question.

MEDITATION MOMENT: As you reflect back over your life, can you identify a hinge moment? Although you might not have recognized it as such at the time, can you now see that God was seeking to move you in a different direction that necessitated a new way of thinking and acting? Describe your hinge moment in as much or as little detail as necessary.

Day 4—The Sign of Scarlet

Yesterday we looked at Rahab's hinge moment. We identified a hinge moment as that point in a person's life when they realize they need to do something different than what they have been doing in order to have a different and better outcome. Who would have thought that in the middle of this storyline, the God of Israel would insert a hidden picture of Christ and his atoning blood? Go back to Joshua 2:12–21.

- In verse 13, what did Rahab ask of the spies?

- What promise did they give her in verse 14?

- What special stipulations were involved in this agreement? In other words, what three things did Rahab promise the men that she would do in order to keep her end of the bargain?

Rahab had to agree to tell no one other than her family about the coming invasion of Jericho by the Israelites. She also had to make certain that all her family members were with her in her home when the invasion occurred. Finally, she had to hang a scarlet cord in her window. In essence, Rahab had to place her faith in these men and their God so that she and her family would be saved. She had only the verbal promise of these two spies that when the Israelite army invaded Jericho, they would do the best they could to protect those in her home. Rahab was truly placing saving faith in an unseen God.

The scarlet cord that Rahab hung in the window signified her trust in God and His agents. Consider another time when a sign of scarlet signified trust in God.

Read Exodus 12:1–13.

- Describe the scarlet sign detailed in this passage.

- Who was instructed to place this sign?

- Why did they need this scarlet sign on their doorposts?

The Israelites were instructed to place the blood of a perfect year old lamb on their doorposts in order to signify their trust in God. When the angel of death swept through Egypt, if he saw the blood on the doorpost, that home would be *passed over* and the first born in that home would not be slain.

Consider, if you will, Warren Wiersbe's commentary on these two separate usages of scarlet signs in the Bible. "In the case of Rahab, the spies instructed her to hang a scarlet rope out of the window of her house, which was built into the wall. This scarlet rope would identify the 'house of safety' to the army of Israel when they came to take the city. The color of the rope is significant for it reminds us of blood. Just as the blood on the doorposts in Egypt marked a house that the angel of death was to pass over, so the scarlet rope marked a house on the Jericho wall whose occupants the Jewish soldiers were to protect."[2]

Some commentators do not agree with Wiersbe that the color of the cord holds significance. My heart tells me it does. Just as Rahab's physical salvation was dependant on the scarlet cord being visible to the Israelite army, so our spiritual salvation is dependent on the blood of Jesus Christ washing over our hearts and providing cleansing from sin.

If I get to heaven and God tells me that I was wrong on this scarlet cord issue…well, it won't be the first thing I will have been wrong about. If that happens, though, I suspect that God will, at the very least, have been pleased that I had the faith to believe a simple red cord was significant in the God-breathed Word.

Trust. Faith. Believing that an unseen God is able to produce a seen result. It is a very important part of the legacy that we leave. To be honest with you, I am amazed at Rahab's faith. This was a pagan prostitute whose only knowledge of the God of Abraham, Isaac and Jacob was hear-say. She had never experienced His awesome power personally. She had never heard that still small voice in her heart. She had never relied on His guiding hand. Yet, she threw herself upon His mercy because she recognized that He was her only hope.

Perhaps there are some similarities between you and Rahab. For me, there are more similarities than I care to admit. But one stands out in bold relief. Each day, I throw myself upon His mercy because I recognize that He is my only hope. My Only Hope. Without Him, I'd be back in a pit of sin so fast, it would make my head spin. He is my only hope for leaving a godly legacy. I tie that scarlet cord of the blood of Jesus Christ in the window of my heart with confident assurance that He will not fail me.

God honored Rahab's trust in Him in at least two ways. In Matthew 1, we are given the geneology of our Lord Jesus Christ, and Rahab's name is tucked away in verse 5. Rahab was the great-great-grandmother of King David. If we continue reading, in Matthew 1:16, we find that ultimately, Jesus was a direct descendant of King David.

In Hebrews 11, the chapter that is commonly referred to as "God's Hall of Faith," we see how God felt about Rahab's trust in Him. Fill in the blanks as you read Hebrews 11:31.

- "By faith the prostitute Rahab, because she welcomed the spies, was not _____ with those who were _____."

Are you building a legacy of faith in God? No matter your history or your current circumstances, if the faith of a prostitute from Jericho can be commended by God in His Holy Word, please know that it is not too late for you to start building a godly legacy. Tie that scarlet cord of faith in the window and wait expectantly for His arrival, my friend.

MEDITATION MOMENT: Spend some time asking God to increase your faith. Ask Him to show you areas where your faith needs some work.

Day 5—Back to Basics

In *Your Churning Place,* Robert Wise shares a story that reminds us that failure can be used by God for good as we walk this dusty road of life.

> I had a friend who used to call me on the phone on Monday mornings. I'd pick up the phone and this minister would say, "Hello, this is God. I have a gift for you today. I want to give you the gift of failing. Today you do not have to succeed. I grant that to you." Then he would hang up. I would sit there for ten minutes, staring at the wall.
>
> The first time I couldn't believe it. It was really the gospel. God's love means it's even okay to fail. You don't have to be the greatest thing in the world. You can just be you.[3]

Yes, my legacy-building friend, you can *just be you.*

Perhaps you are thinking, "Leah, you have no idea what being 'me' looks like. I have messed up so many times that my middle name is 'mistake.'"

No, I don't know what "being you" looks like, but I do know how terribly I have failed over the years that I have walked with Jesus. I also know that making trophies of grace from the trash pile of life is the specialty of Jesus. How do I know that? Because I am a trophy. God loves taking ordinary, failure-prone, repeat-offender humans and turning them into portraits of faith, worthy of being held up as examples for those who follow behind.

The *only* way that we can live a life that leaves a godly legacy for the coming generations is to make Jesus the boss, the king, and the ruler of our lives. We will never be able to live that life without His help. Leaving a godly legacy will not happen through trying harder or doing lots of good things. A life that leaves a godly legacy is based on Jesus Christ and His power to change us from the inside out.

Perhaps your hinge moment is now. You have been living your life being a good person and doing good things, but you have this nagging suspicion that there is more to leaving a godly legacy than what you have been doing. You recognize, like Rahab, when all is said and done, that you have to do something different than what you have been doing in order for your life to really matter.

You may realize that, no matter how good you are or how many good things you do, you are never going to be good enough to get into heaven. I have heard that the definition of insanity is doing the same thing over and over, but expecting a different result. Does that resonate with you? Have you been trying and trying to be good enough to be accepted by God, loved by God? Yet you still feel that you always come up short, and you don't know what to do to change that.

The problem, my friend, is that you have fallen into the trap of believing that you can make yourself acceptable to God—when in fact, none of us can be acceptable to Him without Jesus. So if you are ready to begin living a life that will leave a godly legacy for the generations coming behind you, please take a short trip with me through some Bible verses and allow me to explain God's plan for setting you on the road to a godly legacy.

Read the following verses and fill in the blanks to some key verses that tell us about God's plan for making us fit for His treasure chest.

- Psalm 139:1–2: "O Lord, you have searched me and _____ _____." *God knows you inside and out—completely.*

- Romans 3:23: "For _____have sinned and fall short of the glory of God." *All means you. All means me. None of us measure up to the perfection of God. No one. Our rebellion and disobedience to God's commands is sin.*

- Romans 6:23: "For the wages of sin is _____, but the _____of God is eternal life in Christ Jesus our Lord." *Rebellion and disobedience have consequences, and the consequences according to God are death—separation from God forever and ever.*

- Romans 5:8: "But God demonstrates His own _____ for _____in this; while we were _____sinners, Christ died for us." *God loved you so much that He didn't want you to be separated from Him forever. Since our rebellion required a payment by death, God sent Jesus to die on the cross in your place, paying the fine that you owed for your rebellion and disobedience. He did this long before you ever realized you needed Him to be the boss, the king, and the ruler of your life.*

- Romans 10:9: "That if you confess with your mouth, 'Jesus is Lord,' and _____ in your _____that God raised Him from the dead, you will be saved." *Jesus did the hard work. He died a horrible death on a cross to pay the fine you owed for your rebellion and disobedience. You must ask Him to forgive you of your rebellion and disobedience and allow His death to pay for your sin.*

- Romans 10:13: "For _____who calls on the name of the Lord will be saved." *Anyone who sincerely and honestly asks Jesus to come into their heart and be the boss, the king, and the ruler of their life will find that He is faithful to do that.*

- Hebrews 7:25: "Therefore He is able to save _____those who come to God through Him, because He always lives to _____for them." *Once you ask Jesus to come into your heart and live, He will not only enable you to live a godly life; He will also go to God on your behalf, seeking His best for your life.*

Have you ever asked Jesus to come into your heart and be the boss, the king, and the ruler of your life? If not, today can be your hinge moment! Right now, as you sit before Him, recognizing that you desire to leave a godly legacy but having never taken that first step of asking Him to come into your heart, I encourage you to pray this prayer and ask Him to come live in your heart:

"Dear Jesus, I realize that I cannot build a godly legacy for the generations that come behind me because I have never asked You to be the boss of my life. I recognize that You died on the cross to pay the fine for my sin, and then You rose from the grave to give me life forever with You in heaven. Please forgive me for my rebellion and disobedience. I ask You to come into my heart and be my forever-friend. Help me to live in a way that is pleasing to You; a way that builds a godly legacy for the coming generations. Thank you, Jesus, for never giving up on me. I love You. Amen.

Dear friend, if you prayed that prayer and made those words your very own, Jesus now lives in your heart, and He will help you live a life that will leave a godly legacy for others to see. I am so proud of you. He is so proud of you.

Next week, we will begin looking at the first of three parts of a godly legacy. Until then, bask in the love of your Lord Jesus Christ. Go tell someone what Jesus has done for you. I'll see you next week.

MEDITATION MOMENT: Begin thinking about what you would like for people to remember about you when you leave this earth. When people stand at your memorial service, what do you hope is said about you?

Week 2—Legacy Building Block 1: Faith

In week two, our time will be spent examining if God is really who He says He is. Our faith must have an object, and that object must be the sovereign God who created the universe. Do you believe that He is really the one true God? I will share with you how the Lord tested my faith and how I found Him to be exceedingly faithful in the midst of a trial of monumental proportions. We will study some of the names by which He is called in an effort to gain a bone-marrow-deep understanding that He is worthy of our faith. He will never leave us or forsake us. He wants the best for us and will move heaven and earth to make it happen. In fact, He did move heaven and earth for us. He is God alone!

Week 2 Goals:

- Examine the faith of Joshua and the priests of Israel

- See God's faithfulness in the lives of modern-day believers

- Study the names of God so that we are better able to understand who He is and what He desires to be for us

Day 1—What Is Faith?

Welcome back, my legacy-building friend. I am thrilled that you are with me today. Today we begin thinking through one of the most important parts of our legacy. There are three different parts of our legacy that we will examine over the course of the next four weeks: our faith, our character, and our holiness. This week, we will begin looking at our faith and observe how it is the foundation for building a godly legacy.

It is important that we understand the meaning of faith, and so today I want us to begin by cementing the concept of faith in our minds and hearts. The Greek word that is used for faith in the New Testament is *pistis,* and its definition will add immensely to our study. *Pistis* means "to win over, persuade. Faith, trust, belief. Subjectively, firm persuasion, conviction, belief in the truth, reality, or faithfulness (though rare) of something."[4]

- Turn to Hebrews 11:1 and write out what this verse tells us about faith.

I am particularly drawn to the commentary in the Life Application Bible (NIV) on this verse. "Two words describe faith: *sure* and *certain.* These two qualities need a secure beginning and ending point. The beginning point of faith is believing in God's character—he *is* who he says. The end point is believing in God's promises—he *will* do what he says. When we believe that God will fulfill his promises even though we don't see those promises materializing yet, we demonstrate true faith."[5]

If I were to give you my definition of faith, I would tell you that faith is "knowing that what you know is true." Let's look at an example in the Bible of faith and see what we can learn that would expand our faith.

- Read Joshua 3 and answer the following questions:

    o   The Israelites were camped at the edge of what body of water?

    o   Moses has already died, but in his place God left whom in charge?

    o   What piece of furniture did Joshua instruct the Israelite people to watch and follow?

    o   Who was responsible for carrying the ark?

As we read Joshua 3, we find at least two excellent examples of faith. The first is Joshua, son of Nun, whom the Bible tells us in Joshua 1:1 had been Moses' aide. Joshua had been the right hand man to "*the* man" who had been tapped by God to bring the Israelite nation out from captivity in Egypt. He had seen Moses at his finest, leading the Israelites out of Egypt and across the Red Sea in a miraculous journey. Joshua had probably been present when the manna fell from heaven and the waters were turned from bitter to sweet. Joshua had journeyed with Moses up on Mount Sinai for God to provide the Ten Commandments. He had been witness to the glory of God falling on the wilderness tabernacle as Moses and Aaron presented the completed compound to the Lord. If ever anyone had been in the presence of spiritual royalty, it would have been Joshua.

So many people live under the misconception that because they grew up in church or because their Daddy was a preacher or a deacon or because they were taken to church all their lives, they are automatically granted a spiritually elite status. If such a thing was possible, then Joshua would have been a most excellent candidate.

Joshua, however, could not get by on Moses' faith. He had to come to a place where he made a decision that he knew what he knew about God was true. Joshua made that decision early in his life as he trained under Moses. Did he live his life by faith? You bet he did.

- Read Joshua 24:15 and note what Joshua proclaimed in faith.

The priests who carried the ark are a second example of faith. Return to Joshua 3 and read verses 14–17 again.

Did you really get what it said? Picture the scene with me. It is springtime in Israel, and more than one million people are standing breathlessly at the edge of the Jordan River. The rainy season has turned a normally tranquil river into a swollen, raging ribbon of rapids. At its widest point, the Jordan would have been approximately one mile across. This was a no-way-across, no-win situation. The people appeared to be stuck on the side of the river opposite the Promised Land.

Into the picture steps the living God. He instructs Joshua to tell the priests to pick up the most holy piece of furniture ever made—the Ark of the Covenant—and begin moving forward toward the edge of the Jordan. Those men had to be thinking, "Has Joshua lost his mind? Is he blind? Can he not see that we are going to be washed away the moment we step foot in this river?" Yet Scripture records not one murmur of dissent from the priests. Why? They had a history with the God of Abraham, Isaac, and Jacob and knew He could be trusted. They had seen God's hand at work in their lives. They had watched Him deliver their people countless times. They knew that He was exactly who He said He was—and if He desired for them to march into a swollen, raging river, then that is exactly what they would do.

- In Joshua 3:15–16, what are we told happened as soon as the priest's feet touched the edge of the Jordan?

- Fill in the blank from Joshua 3:17: The priests who carried the ark of the covenant of the Lord stood firm on _____ in the middle of the Jordan.

Hear this amazing verse from *The Message:* "And there they stood; those priests carrying the Chest of the Covenant stood firmly planted on dry ground in the middle of the Jordan while all Israel crossed on dry ground. Finally the whole nation was across the Jordan, and not one wet foot."[6]

That, my friend, is an amazing picture of the results and rewards of faith. Those priests knew that God was the creator of all things, including that swollen, raging Jordan River. They knew that their sole purpose in life was to serve and obey God—and if that meant stepping into a river that could drown them, then they were willing to take the risk in order to be obedient.

You see, it is only in the exercising of faith that faith grows. If the priests had decided that their fear was larger than their faith, they would have missed the opportunity to not only see God do the miraculous, but to be part of that miracle. It was only when they stepped into the river by faith that the God of their faith stepped out and showed off. No mud was on the feet of the priests. God not only cleared the way for the priests carrying the ark and the people of the nation of Israel to go across the Jordan, but he did it in a way that assured they knew that it was all about Him. No mud. Clean feet. It was surely a God thing!

Faith—it's being sure of what you hope for and certain of what you do not see. What are you hoping for? Down deep in your heart, what hope are you carrying around? Could it be that God is waiting for you to submerge your feet in the waters and prove that you know that He is who He says He is and that you trust Him completely?

MEDITATION MOMENT: Spend some time journaling your thoughts and prayers regarding the thing or things that you are hoping for. Ask God to show you clearly if you need to take a step of faith in order for Him to roll back the waters and show off on your behalf.

Day 2—A Faith Tested

On December 18, 2002, I was working in my office at home, anticipating a telephone call from my mother informing me that my daddy had come through his colonoscopy fine and he had a clean bill of health. He had been having some odd symptoms with his gastrointestinal tract, but he had always had problems with his stomach, and I anticipated that the explanation would be a simple one.

At 10:00 that morning, the call came in. I could tell immediately by the tone of my mother's voice that the news was not good. She informed me that the colonoscopy had shown a large tumor that was almost completely obstructing the gastrointestinal tract. Daddy was being prepped for surgery at that moment. I told my mother that I would be to the hospital as soon as I could get there, which would be a little over an hour's drive.

I arrived just prior to the attendant wheeling Daddy out of the room toward the surgery suite. During the three-hour surgery, I kept telling myself that this would be something that we could deal with, and everything would be all right. The control freak in me was assessing the situation from every possible angle in anticipation of being able to make everything easy and manageable. The only angle I forgot to include was what the doctor told us when he came to Daddy's room after surgery.

With a grim face, he told us that he had removed the tumor along with a portion of my dad's colon. In addition, they had done some exploratory surgery while in the abdomen, and they found three spots of cancer on Daddy's liver. The doctor was not sure if surgery would be beneficial and was referring Daddy to a doctor in Atlanta at Emory for further evaluation.

Whoosh! DID. NOT. SEE. THAT. ONE. COMING!! Because of my medical training, I knew that what we were dealing with was *not* good. This would not be easy, and it might not even be manageable. I was in way over my Miss-Clairol-Steamy-Cappuccino colored head with this one. This is one situation over which I had no control—*none*.

Soon after Daddy was brought back to his room, I told him I loved him, kissed him goodbye, and drove the hour back across the mountain to my home. On the way back, the Lord and I had a chat. Here is how it went:

"Lord, what in the world?" I asked. "Why would you allow this? Daddy loves you and follows you. He has suffered so much in his life from having polio. Why?"

"Leah, do you really believe that I am who I say I am?" God answered.

"Yes, Lord, I do."

"Leah, do you truly believe that I love your daddy far more than you could ever love him?"

Pausing and thinking, I responded, "Well, yes, I suppose so, Lord."

"Do you believe that I will do what is best for your Daddy—and do you think I need your help dealing with this?"

"I suppose you will, Lord—and I guess you do not need my help."

"Then trust Me with your daddy."

19

In the moment that I surrendered control of this situation to the Lord, an unexplainable peace flooded my soul. Little did I know that my family and I were about to take a journey with the Lord that would result in a deepening of our individual faith—or that it would be unlike anything we had ever experienced.

For the remainder of this week, I want us to explore God's character and determine if we can boldly proclaim that He is who He says He is. My hope is that this exercise will help us do one of two things. It will assist us in either cementing an already-growing faith into the legacy that we leave, or pushing us to begin a relationship with God whereby our faith is rooted and grounded in Him and His Word.

First, let's consider God's character—who He is. Read the following verses and note what they tell you about God's character by filling in the blanks.

- Psalm 62:11–12: "One thing God has spoken, two things have I heard: that you, O God, are _____, and that you, O Lord, are _____."

- Psalm 103:8: "The Lord is _____ and _____, slow to _____, abounding in _____."

- Isaiah 35:4: "Say to those with fearful hearts, 'Be strong, do not fear; your God will come, he will come with _____; with divine retribution he will come to save you.'"

- Jeremiah 32:17: "Ah, Sovereign Lord, you have made the heavens and the earth by your great _____ and outstretched arm. _____ is too _____ for you."

- Zephaniah 3:17: "The Lord your God is with you, he is _____ to save. He will take great _____ in you, he will quiet you with his _____, he will _____ over you with _____."

- Philippians 4:19: "And my God will _____ all your _____ according to his glorious riches in Christ Jesus."

- 2 Timothy 2:13: "If we are faithless, He will remain _____, for he cannot disown himself."

In this group of verses, we learn much about God's character. We learn that He is strong and loving, compassionate and gracious, slow to get angry, and full of love. He is mighty and powerful. He delights in us and rejoices over us. He makes it His business to know our needs and meet them in His time. Above all, He is faithful to us—even when we are grossly unfaithful.

Tomorrow we will continue our examination of the character of God as we try to decide if He is a God who is worthy of our faith—a God whose character we would like to reflect as we seek to build a legacy for the coming generations.

MEDITATION MOMENT: Which of God's character attributes that we studied today do you most need to experience in your relationship with Him? Which of these attributes do you need Him to work in and through you so that you can begin building a godly legacy?

Day 3—He Will Never Forsake You

Ask almost any woman whether they would rather feel secure or respected and you will find that an overwhelming number will tell you they would rather feel secure. Why? Well, the main reason would have to be that God designed us that way. It is only my theory, but let me give it to you anyway. I think our need for security is what drives women to a relationship with God so much easier than men. Women, in general, don't seem to mind appearing to need God or to be dependent on Him; whereas so often, men live with a false bravado and seem to feel that it is okay to have God in their lives as long as it doesn't cause them to get to where it is obvious that they *need* Him in their lives. I'm not saying this is true for all men and women, but for a huge portion of society, it seems to fit.

Today as we continue our examination into the character of God, let's seek out evidence for His ability to provide security for us.

- • Read the following verses and circle the concept that is repeated in each verse: Deuteronomy 31:6, Deuteronomy 31:8, Joshua 1:5, Isaiah 41:17, and Hebrews 13:5

  A) God will always love us   B) God will never forsake us

  C) God will deal justly with us   D) God will quiet us with His love

The thought of being forsaken or abandoned is one that strikes fear in the heart of adults and children alike. Most of us can probably recall a time when we felt abandoned or forsaken, either by a person, a job, or something else. Being forsaken or abandoned causes you to feel as if you have very little worth in the eyes of the person doing the abandoning. The self-esteem of a person who has been abandoned is damaged horribly. Their personal sense of security is completely destroyed, and they often have trouble trusting again in a similar relationship.

Allow me to share a story from the life of my friend, Kathie, about being abandoned by a human, yet loved and securely held by God. It is my honor to have Kathie share her story in her own words.

> My story begins as a naïve eighteen-year-old missionary kid, recently returned from overseas. You can imagine that life choices were not a strong suit, as we never really had choices to make for ourselves growing up. I soon met the love of my life … the man who on my nineteenth birthday would become my husband. This man was my soul mate—which, in looking back, should have been the first red flag. Shouldn't Christ alone be our soul mate?
>
> But there you have it—at nineteen, I married, and shortly after my twentieth birthday had a wonderful son. The honeymoon lasted about two months—two months of happiness; two months together seeking out God's will for our lives; two months of working to heal the wounds my husband carried from years of abandonment, foster care, and loss. But then those wounds took over, and seeking solace from the pain of the abandonment he carried, he did the only thing he knew to do—run. Our lives became a roller coaster of his leaving and coming home, his abuse of alcohol, and later drugs—and me. During the first of his many disappearances, I learned I was pregnant. I finally found him and told him of the baby, asking if he would come

home, if we could work things out. A week later, he returned, only to continue the cycle of running, abuse, and alcoholism.

Amazingly, he was there for the birth of our child, and how proud he was. The few pictures I have of him include a few of the proud father holding his son—a son named for him. But even this child could not heal the wounds he carried from a life of loss, and soon the cycle of abuse began again. The marriage soon ended in divorce after threats to take our son and leave left me fearful for the safety of our small child.

Eventually, his journey to reconnect with his birth family took him to California. I never really knew where he was living in California, although I often prayed for healing, for reconciliation, for relief for his pain and my own.

The ultimate pain came one morning when I was awakened by the phone ringing at 6:00 am. It was him—his voice filled with joy, he told me his life was coming together. He told me of his Las Vegas wedding the night before to the love of his life, and ultimately he told me they had a son, a son he considered to be his first born.

We no longer existed; we were part of his past that he had successfully excised. As I hung up the phone, I looked across the room where my son slept and began to cry. *Cry* is such a small word for the grief that followed—a grief that I knew only the Lord could understand. A grief that left my mind in a fog and my body lifeless except for the racking sobs that escaped me. I did the only thing I knew to do. I couldn't pray. I couldn't organize my thoughts well enough to utter the stilted sentences I grew up hearing as prayer. All I could do was cry out with my very soul to the Christ I knew had hung on the cross for me. The only words I could utter (and I am not sure they were actually uttered or if my spirit simply flung them into the heavens) were, "Lord, hold me!"

Only two times in my life have I been given the gift of the physical reality of spiritual comfort. This night was one of them. As I cried out to the Lord, I physically felt the Spirit around me; the comfort was not fleeting, but rather insistent and strong as I felt arms wrap around my sobbing shoulders. The sobs did not stop right away—instead the comfort allowed the sobs to release the pain of loss and abandonment.

While I may have been abandoned by my human love, Christ's love reached through all my mistakes and poor choices to give comfort that has never been forgotten. Christ doesn't withhold his love until we get it together; *His* love and comfort is there, waiting for us, ready to step in even when we don't know how to call to Him. He is there.

As my friend's story make so beautifully clear, even when our world seems to fall apart, God is there, and He never abandons us. In Ezekiel 48:35, we are reminded that one of the names by which God is called is *Jehovah shammah.*

- Read this verse and write out what *Jehovah shammah* means: "The Lord is _____."

Dear friend, if you have accepted Jesus as your Lord and Savior, God will never abandon you; He will never forsake you. In your lowest moment, you may not be able to feel His presence—but make no mistake, He is there. He never leaves you, He never takes a break, He never takes a nap. He is there, right beside you, always working in your life. A treasure chest legacy believes that even when there is no physical evidence to fuel our faith, God is right beside us each moment of our lives!

MEDITATION MOMENT: As you reflect back over your life, think about times when you felt as though God had abandoned you, yet in retrospect you know that He was walking with you all the while. Thank Him that He never forsakes or abandons you.

Day 4—What's His Name?

In the marvelous book *Same Kind of Different As Me,* Ron Hall and Denver Moore tell the story of how their lives intersected and how each was never the same afterward. Ron and his wife, Debbie, began volunteering at a mission for the homeless in Texas, and it was at this mission that they met Denver. Denver had lived homeless on the streets for many years after fleeing a life of modern day slavery on a cotton plantation in the south.

On the first day that Debbie and Ron volunteered at the mission, Debbie asked all the homeless people their names because she desired to connect with them through the calling them of their names. Later on in the book, after working at the mission many times, Ron takes Denver to a coffee shop in an attempt to get to know him better and develop a friendship. In the course of the time in the coffee shop, the following conversation takes place:

> Suddenly, Denver dropped his head and became silent. 'What is it?" I said, concerned I might have pushed too hard. He raised his head and stared into my eyes, his own like brown lasers locked on target. In my mind, I started counting to one hundred and was past eighty when he finally spoke.
>
> "Mind if I ask you a personal question?" he said.
>
> "Of course not. Ask me anything you want."
>
> "I don't wanna make you mad, and you don't have to tell me nothing if you don't want to."
>
> "Ask away," I said and braced myself.
>
> Again, a long pause. Then softly: "What's your name?"
>
> "What's my name! That's what you wanted to ask me?"
>
> "Yessir …" he ventured, embarrassment creeping up his cheeks. "In the circle I live in, you don't ask nobody his name."
>
> Suddenly, I flashed back to the slack-jawed stares we'd encountered on our first day at the mission. *You don't ask nobody his name ….*[7]

As we continue to consider the character of God and whether He is really who He says He is, let's take some time to examine some of the names that He has willingly shared with us. God desires for us to know Him intimately, and He is called by at least sixteen different names in the Old Testament, each of those names divulging to us a new aspect of His character. So lick your fingers and get ready to take a whirlwind tour through the Old Testament as we explore God's character by learning a few of His names.

Elohim

This name for God describes His power and His might. We find this name, Elohim, used in many places—but most notably in Genesis 1:1 (NKJV): "In the beginning God [Elohim] created the heavens and the earth."

- What act of God is being described here that would require power and might?

- As we examine our faith in light of this name of God, is there any situation in your life currently that would require *more* of Elohim's power than it took to create the heavens and the earth? Probably not. There may be a situation, however, where you need Elohim's power to be evidenced. If this is the case, briefly describe it. Be discreet if disclosure would harm another person.

- Are you able to acknowledge Him and place your faith in Elohim, the God of power and might, the Creator of the universe, the one who controls all things? If not, why not?

El-Roi

Often in life, we may feel that no one sees or cares about our troubles and trials. We may feel that if God exists, He certainly does not seem to care about what is going on in the average person's life. He seems too busy handling the really big problems of the world. Have you ever felt like this? If so, please let me introduce you to El-Roi: the God who *sees*. In Genesis 16, an abused and mistreated servant girl, Hagar, has fled out into the wilderness to escape her mistress, Sarai. Sarai had forced Hagar to sleep with her husband, Abram, in order to provide an heir for Abram. When Sarai found out that Hagar was pregnant, she began to hate her and abuse her. Hagar's position in the world would be almost as low as one could get in antiquity, so imagine her surprise when an angel of the Lord found her and began speaking to her about her future. Read Genesis 16:7–16.

- Fill in the blanks with Hagar's words from Genesis 16:13: "She gave this name to the Lord who spoke to her: 'You are the God who _____,' for she said, 'I have now seen the One who _____ _____.'"

- Is there a situation in your life that causes you to feel that no one sees or cares about you? Briefly describe it here.

El-Roi sees you and loves you completely.

Jehovah Jireh

Sometimes as we walk through life with the Lord, He asks us to do something that seems impossible. The thing he requires of us might seem too difficult, too great an expectation. It is in these seasons that God is often testing our faith to see if we truly believe that He is who He says He is.

God did this very thing in Genesis 22 when he tested Abraham's faith by asking him to offer his only son, Isaac, as a sacrifice back to God. In complete obedience and apparently without questioning God (can you imagine it?), Abraham prepared to do the very thing God required. As Abraham bound his son, laid him on the altar, and raised the knife to plunge into his precious son's chest, God called out to him at the last moment and stopped Abraham from killing his son. Instead of Isaac being killed as the sacrifice to God, a ram which was caught in the thicket by its horn was offered on the altar.

- Genesis 22:14 records what Abraham said after he offered the sacrifice of the ram on the altar. Fill in the blank: "So Abraham called that place The Lord will _____ _____. And to this day it is said, 'On the mountain of the Lord it will be _____.'"

- Is there a situation in your life where you desperately need God's provision?

It could be that you need material provision, spiritual provision, or physical provision. Jehovah Jireh will always *provide* exactly what you need as you are obedient to what He asks of you. His provision may be very different from what you asked or expected, but it will always be designed to grow your faith and bring glory to Him.

Jehovah Shalom

We live in a world that is nearly devoid of peace. Our governments seek peace and make war. Our families need peace, yet conflict is often the order of the day. Our hearts long for peace, searching for it in so many places—so many inappropriate places.

In Judges 6:24, we find young Gideon being asked by an angel of the Lord to rise up, be bold, and lead Israel to victory over the Midianites who were oppressing the Israelites horribly. God had allowed this oppression of the Israelites in order to open their eyes to their own sin and idolatry. The people had brought this season of oppression on themselves, and the only way they would find relief from it was to admit their sin, turn from it, and follow only God.

Gideon recognized—with the help of the angel of the Lord—that true peace would only come through God. At the same time, he was frightened because of the visit of the angel. Read Judges 6:22–24 and see how the angel calms Gideon's fears.

- What did the angel of the Lord say to Gideon in response to his exclamation that he had seen the Lord?

- What did Gideon call the altar he had built to the Lord?

- Perhaps there is a place in your life where you need Jehovah Shalom to provide His *peace.* Describe the situation and write a short prayer asking God to give you His peace and wisdom about the situation you described.

Jehovah Shammah

Finally, we come to a name of God that speaks volumes to me. We glanced at this name yesterday, but let's think about it once again. How often do we waste time pondering on and worrying about situations in our lives over which we have no control? It could be something that we are currently dealing with or something that we anticipate might occur in the future. We get ourselves all worked up over it, worrying ourselves almost sick at times; yet we can do nothing about it—nothing to change it, nothing to prevent it, nothing.

Enter into a session of true confession with me and allow me to share an example with you. I am typically not a fearful person; I never have been. I face life head-on and rarely shy away from conflict. There is one thing, however, of which I am fearful (other than snakes!)—I am fearful of and dread growing old. I do not fear death, but I do fear growing old and sick.

As I have become more honest and vulnerable with the Lord about this fear, He has been so faithful to provide reminders to me that He is already in that moment which I dread so terribly. He is Jehovah Shammah. He has promised to walk with me through it and provide for me. *He is there*—Jehovah Shammah.

As we saw yesterday, this name of God is found in Ezekiel 48:35 and is used in the context of God establishing Himself in the city of Jerusalem. After the Israelites had experienced exile and a separation from the holy city of Jerusalem, God wanted them to know—without a doubt—that He was present in Jerusalem and He was on His throne.

- Describe a situation that causes you great concern or worry.

- Read Ezekiel 48:35 and fill in the blanks as you pray this short prayer. "Lord, you know this situation that causes me great angst. I ask you to remind me that you are Jehovah Shammah: the Lord is _____. You are already there, in the midst of my worry and anxiety. Help me to find comfort and peace knowing that when I cannot change a circumstance, I can always find peace in knowing that you are in the middle of that circumstance."

Today we have examined several different aspects of God's character in hopes that we will find Him to be exactly who He says He is. We have seen Him as the mighty and powerful God of creation, Elohim. He has revealed Himself as El Roi, the God who sees every one of His children as they go about their daily lives. Jehovah Jireh, the Lord our provider, sees every need that we have and is able to meet them. In a world that lacks peace, Jehovah shalom is our peace if only we will call upon Him and finally, Jehovah Shammah, is there in our todays and our tomorrows.

MEDITATION MOMENT: Take a moment to reflect on the names of God we studied today. Which of these names of God presents the greatest challenge to your faith with regard to really believing that He is that name? How could understanding more about God's character through examining His names build your faith and impact the legacy you leave for the generations that come behind you?

Day 5—Is God Who He Says He Is?

Today is an important day of our Bible study. I hope you have carved out time to spend with me and ponder the issue of whether God is who He says He is. Until you truly believe that God is all that we have studied this week and so much more, you will never walk in the kind of faith that is required to build a godly legacy. Oh, you may have accepted Jesus as your Savior and have assurance of eternal life, but until you are prepared to completely trust the Lord in every area of your life, you will not have a vibrant, peculiar life that causes others to desire what you have in your relationship with Christ.

Allow me to illustrate this truth using an ordinary object that you probably have in your home. If you have a book of matches or a lighter, stop reading right now and go get them. I'll wait right here for you.

Good, you are back. I hope you found the matches or lighter. Take a look at what you are holding. Matches are used to ignite a fire; to bring a flame to life. It is not until you take one out, believing in faith that the match will do what it is designed to do, and strike it against the strip on the book or box, that a flame is produced. As long as it is in the box or pack and unused, it is still a match or a lighter, but it is not being used to its full potential. Now, strike the match or the lighter, producing a flame. Once you strike it and produce a flame it is capable of incredible things—both good and damaging. Perhaps we are a bit frightened of what the match can do—and rightly so. If we are wise, we are very careful with it.

- Read Deuteronomy 4:24 and Hebrews 12:28–29. What is God called in these verses?

God is a bit like a match. Many of us know about Him, and we may even have a relationship with Him because we have placed our trust in Jesus as our Lord and Savior. The problem we have is that we do not fully understand Him. We cannot package God in a box that we can control and understand. This can cause us to be frightened or wary of Him, so we distance ourselves from Him.

It is only when we fully rely upon and believe in Him that He becomes immeasurably more than we will ever need or want. He becomes that consuming fire in whom we can wholly trust and on whom we can fully rely. When we truly believe that God is who He says He is, our faith blooms and we trust Him to do what is best for us, no matter what He allows into our lives.

So let's take some time to review what we have learned about God this week. What follows is the "CliffsNotes" version of our entire week of study. There will be some questions for you to answer, so be prepared to flip back to each day of study to find the answers if needed.

Day 1

On Day 1, we examined the faith of Joshua and the priests who carried the Ark of the Covenant into the Jordan River and watched as God rolled back the waters in response to their faith. Joshua had given the Israelites specific instructions about how to know what to do when the time came to cross the river in Joshua 3:3–4.

- In Joshua 3:3, what was to be the sign that the people were ready to move across the Jordan?

- Verse 4 gives us the reason why the people were to follow the priests and the Ark. Fill in the blanks: "Then you will know which way to go, since you have _____ _____ this _____ before."

My friend, when God sends us on a journey, He will never fail to provide guidance for our feet. Never! I heard it said that God's will is not a roadmap, but a flashlight. It won't show you all the way home tonight, just the next turn in the road. God can be trusted to take us where we need to be and to get us there safely, with no mud on our feet.

Day 2

In addition to God's willingness to guide us, we learned on Day 2 that He is strong, mighty, powerful, and that nothing is too hard for Him. He meets all our needs and is faithful to us; yet to those who harm His children or do not bow to Him as God, He will be a divine judge, seeking vengeance. The Bible also told us that He has a gentle side to His nature. We discovered that He is loving, compassionate, gracious, slow to get angry, and of all things, He sings over us in delight, just like a mother would sing over her child.

God longs for us to trust Him and walk with Him in complete faith. Before Adam and Eve decided to take matters into their own hands, their relationship with God was one that was close and intimate.

- Genesis 2:15 tells us that God took the man and _____ him in _____ of _____.

- Then in Genesis 3:8, we are told that the man and the woman heard the sound of the Lord God as He was _____ in the garden in the cool of the day.

I don't think it is a theological stretch to assume that God might have made walks in the garden a habit. I also can easily picture God inviting Adam and Eve to walk with Him. What we see here is fellowship of the most intimate kind between the Creator and His prized creation. God did not *need* that fellowship. He is self-sustaining and needs nothing. I believe that God desired that fellowship with the man and woman. He wanted them to trust Him completely and rely on Him for all their needs, just as He desires for you and me to trust and rely on Him totally.

Day 3

In Day 3, we saw that God will never leave us or forsake us. Even when we *feel* alone, He is still there, working in the shadows. He is our Jehovah shammah.

Day 4

Day 4 gave us the privilege of getting to know God by learning about some of the names by which He is called in scripture. We learned that He is Elohim, the God of power and might. He is El-Roi, the

God who sees us in every situation in which we find ourselves. As Jehovah Jireh, He is the God who provides for all our needs. He brings peace into our lives in the midst of and in spite of circumstances as our Jehovah shalom.

After examining the character of God and the way that He loves you, I hope that you are able to declare that indeed, God is who He says He is. When you and I can say that from the depths of our hearts, our faith is pleasing to God.

MEDITATION MOMENT: As we have examined whether we believe that God is who He says he is, do you sense your faith growing stronger? Are you prepared to say to Him, "I trust you, Lord, because you have been faithful to so many people, and I believe that you will be faithful to me"? If you cannot yet say this, spend some time journaling and talking to God about the things that are preventing you from fully trusting Him. Talk to a Christian friend, Sunday school teacher, or pastor about your hesitancy to trust God.

Week 3—Promise-Keeping

"I promise." These two words can evoke a multitude of feelings such as security, insecurity, trust, mistrust, joy, or fear. The feelings that the words "I promise" bring forth have their roots in the experiences that we have had with the person making the promise. If people have, by and large, kept their promises to us, then we are likely to believe that what a person promises will happen. Conversely, if we have a history of being the recipient of broken promises, the words "I promise" evoke feelings of mistrust and insecurity.

This week, our journey will take us to a place where we will meet the ultimate promise-keeper—God Himself. We will have the opportunity to decide for ourselves if He truly does keep the promises He makes by examining the lives of those to whom He made promises. Our time together this week will also give us an opportunity for great introspection to see if we, ourselves, find God worthy of our trust.

Week 3 Goals:

- Consider the importance of promise-keeping as described in the Bible

- Examine the promises that God made to Abraham and David and assess His faithfulness to His promises

- Examine the promises that God made about Jesus. Was God faithful to keep those promises?

- Discover what promises God has made to you as a believer in Jesus Christ

Day 1—Promises, Promises

In the early 1980s, the pop duo Naked Eyes made the song "Promises, Promises" popular. In it, the singer laments over the fact that someone made promises to him that they had no intention of keeping. Recall the lyrics with me:

You made me promises, promises
Knowing I'd believe
Promises, promises
You knew you'd never keep

Second time around
I'm still believing words that you said
You said you'd always be here
"In love forever"
Still repeats in my head
You can't finish what you start
If this is love, it breaks my heart

You made me promises, promises
You knew you'd never keep
Promises, promises
Why do I believe [8]

Whether we have experienced the hurt of a broken promise in a romantic relationship, work relationship, or other type of relationship, there are likely few of us who cannot identify with this kind of pain. Broken promises can be emblazoned on our hearts for the rest of our lives. I read of one woman whose parents promised a trip to Florida to her as a child; however, they never told her *when* the trip would take place. Financial difficulties hit her family, and the promised trip never transpired—yet more than twenty years later, this woman remembers that unkept promise made to her by her parents. Broken promises hurt!

Today I want us to continue examining our faith as it relates to the legacy that we are leaving for those who come behind. Let's take a moment to revisit the quote from my NIV Study Bible, which is our foundation for last week's study as well as this week's:

"Two words describe faith: *sure* and *certain*. These two qualities need a secure beginning and ending point. The beginning point of faith is believing in God's character—he *is* who he says. The end point is believing in God's promises—he *will* do what he says. When we believe that God will fulfill his promises even though we don't see those promises materializing yet, we demonstrate true faith."[9]

This week, our goal is to mine a few of the promises of God and evaluate His faithfulness to keep those promises. Is He a promise-keeper worthy of our trust and faith? In life, if we can establish a pattern of faithfulness to promise-keeping in a person, we are more inclined to trust them. Join me in the Word this week as we explore God's promises and whether He has been faithful to keep them.

- In Psalm 145:13, we find a statement that is very matter-of-fact. Choose the word that fits in the blank in order to complete this statement: "Your kingdom is an everlasting kingdom, and your dominion endures through all generations. The Lord is faithful to _____ His promises and loving toward all he has made."

  Some of   A Few of   Most of   All   None of

The words *promise* or *promises* are used ninety-five times in the Word of God. This appears to be an important concept, since God saw fit to have it included in His Word in many significant places. Let's take a look at just a few of them.

- Match the scripture with what it says about a promise or promises:

Joshua 21:45	God's promises allow us to live the divine life
Romans 15:8	God remembered his holy promise to Abraham
2 Corinthians 1:20	God kept *every* promise He made to Israel
2 Peter 3:9	God is not slow in keeping His promises, but patient
2 Peter 1:4	God is not a man who breaks His promises
Numbers 23:19	Jesus—fulfillment of God's promise to the patriarchs
2 Samuel 7:25	God has power to do what He has promised
Psalm 105:42	Jesus is the "yes" to all of God's promises
Romans 4:21	In faith, David asked God to keep His promises

Because of the limitations of our human minds, it is difficult—if not downright impossible—for us to comprehend a Being who can make promises and *always* keep them. We have no mental or emotional file drawer for that kind of promise-keeping ability, because it is impossible in the human realm. As hard as we try to keep the promises that we have made, we will, at some point, fail to keep a promise.

We make promises that we cannot keep because we do not have an eternal perspective. We have no way to know if our health, our finances, our circumstances, or any one of a million other things will prevent us from keeping a promise that we make. Our best intentions are subject to so many external and internal forces that can cause us to break a promise.

God, on the other hand, is not constrained or compelled by earthly and fleshly influences. He is able to keep every promise He makes, because He is not subject to human weakness, and He also has the eternal perspective that enables Him to make promises that are worth keeping.

- Take a moment to go back and look at the promises you just matched with the corresponding verses. Circle the promise that means the most to you personally and write below why that promise holds special meaning to you.

Let's go again to Numbers 23:19 and be reminded of this very concept. This time, however, I will give it to you from *The Message*. Allow these words to soak into your heart as you read them: "God is not man, one given to lies, and not a son of man changing his mind. Does he speak and not do what he says? Does he promise and not come through?"[10]

It is only when we learn to completely trust God that we will be able to fully surrender to His will and His plan. As that happens, our legacy of faith is built for those who come behind us.

God keeps His promises, as you will see throughout the course of this week of study. You did well in your study today. Rest in the knowledge that your time spent in the Word is smiled upon by God. He promises to bless and multiply your efforts.

MEDITATION MOMENT: Is there a promise that someone made to you at some point in your life that they were unable to keep, and did their failure to keep that promise hurt you deeply? Have you forgiven that person for not keeping their promise to you? If not, ask God to help you forgive that person. If you have forgiven them, stop and pray that God will help you to make wise promises that you can keep.

Day 2 – God's Promise to Abraham

On January 17, 1995, surrounded by family and friends, I stood in the Susan B. Harris Chapel on the campus of Young Harris College in Young Harris, Georgia and promised to be a faithful wife to my husband, Greg, until death separated us. So often our promises have far-reaching—often eternal—implications, and nowhere is this more true than in the marriage relationship. We promised to love, honor, and cherish each other before God and our families. I fear that more often than we care to admit, we have failed to do what we promised. Not because the other didn't deserve it, but because we simply chose otherwise. There have been times when we failed to keep our promises to each other. By God's grace, these failures have not been ones that resulted in fatal fractures in our marriage. Yet we are wise to continually keep those promises in mind.

God made a promise to Abraham (then known as Abram). Today we will examine that promise and determine if God was able to fulfill what He had promised. It is important that we understand a bit about Abram before we look at the promise.

Abram, as far as we can tell, did not have a prior history with God. He bursts onto the scene in Genesis 11 as a descendant of Shem, one of the sons of Noah. We are told in Joshua 24:2 that Abram's people were an idol-worshipping people from the land of Ur of the Chaldeans. Why would God strike a deal with a man who had a family history of worshipping idols? What made Abram special enough that God would call him out and use him, promising to make him a great and mighty nation?

I suspect we find the reason in Genesis 12. I believe that it had a great deal to do with his heart of obedience. Abraham's willingness to follow God without knowing or understanding God's plan was a crucial starting point for the legacy of faith and obedience that Abraham would leave for the generations that came behind him. Examine this passage with me.

Answer the following questions based on Genesis 12:1–4:

- In verse 1, what things did God ask Abram to leave?

- Where did God instruct Abram to go?

- In verses 2 and 3a, we find the five "I will" promises that God made to Abram. Write them here.

- In the final part of verse 3, we find God summarizing His promise in a statement that has reverberated through the ages with meaning and power. Write out the last part of verse 3.

- What does verse 4 tell us that Abram did after the Lord gave him these promises?

Abram left. He didn't question or quarrel. He simply got up in obedience and left. This, I believe, is why God chose to make Abraham the recipient of magnificent promises.

Briefly, let's examine the "I will" promises in verses 2 and 3 and verify whether or not God kept His promises to Abram.

"I will make you into a great nation."

God's first "I will" promise to Abram was to make him into a great nation. Abraham fathered Isaac, and Isaac fathered Jacob. Jacob was the father of men who ultimately became the patriarchs of the twelve tribes of Israel. Skip forward several generations, and we find in Exodus 1 that the people who made up the twelve tribes of Israel were "exceedingly numerous," according to Exodus 1:7. After 400 years of slavery in Egypt, the Israelites left Egypt under the leadership of Moses. As they journeyed out of Egypt, we are told in Exodus 12:37 that the number of the Israelite men were about six _____ _____, not counting women and children. Did God keep His promise to make Abram into a great nation? Yes, he did. More than a million people is definitely my idea of a great nation.

"I will bless you, and I will make your name great."

Next, God promised to bless Abram and make his name great. The Hebrew word that is used in the second "I will" promise for bless is *barak,* and it means "to bless, to praise, be blessed." Throughout the Bible, the name of Abraham is praised, and even today, the Jewish people honor Abraham the patriarch. Throughout the Bible, God is known as the God of Abraham, Isaac, and Jacob. God blessed Abraham with two sons, Ishmael and Isaac. It was through Isaac that the Messiah, Jesus Christ, would come to this earth. Yes, God certainly blessed Abraham and made his name great.

- Read Genesis 17:3–8 and list the ways that God promised to bless Abraham and make his name great.

"I will bless those who bless you, and I will curse those who curse you."

In His next two "I will" promises, God promised to bless those who blessed Abram and curse those who cursed Abram. Did God keep these promises? Let's do some investigative work and find out.

The Israelites were held captive as slaves in Egypt for 400 years, during which time they were mistreated and suffered greatly. When Pharaoh refused to let them leave, God sent ten plagues on the Egyptians to try to convince them to allow the Israelites to leave. The tenth plague was the one that would ultimately cause Pharaoh to send the Israelites fleeing out into the desert.

- Read Exodus 11:1–8. Record what Moses told Pharaoh would occur because of his persecution of the Israelites.

In these verses, Scripture is very careful to draw a distinction between the Egyptians and the Israelites. Verse 7 tells us that not even a dog would bark at an Israelite during this time of death of the firstborn, despite the fact that there would be death, destruction, and wailing in every Egyptian household. God would make it very clear that only Egyptians were affected by this plague.

When Pharaoh discovered that, indeed, every Egyptian home was affected horribly by this plague of death of the firstborn, he and the Egyptian people were eager to see the Israelites leave Egypt.

- In a dramatic reversal of fortune, the Word of God allows us a moment to celebrate with the Israelites as they leave Egypt. Read Exodus 12:35–36 and note what the Israelites carried out of Egypt.

The plunder that the Israelites carried out of Egypt provided the materials they needed to one day build the wilderness tabernacle where they would worship the one true God. Amazing!

God cursed those who cursed Abraham's descendants. What about blessing those who blessed them? Do you remember our study of Rahab, the prostitute from Jericho, who aided the Israelite spies in their scouting mission into Jericho? She is a classic example of God blessing those who blessed Israel. Despite her questionable background, Rahab became an ancestor of King David and ultimately the Lord Jesus Christ.

If you are a believer of Jesus Christ, *you* are evidence that God kept His promise to Abraham. How, you ask? In Romans 4:16–17 we are told by the apostle Paul that we are all children of Abraham, whether we are Jewish or Gentile. We who are Gentiles are the children of Abraham because of our faith. See this with me.

- Fill in the blanks in the following verses:

    o Romans 4:3: Abraham _____ God, and it was credited to him as righteousness.

    o Romans 4:6: David says the same thing when he speaks of the blessedness of the _____ to whom God credits righteousness apart from works.

    o Romans 4:9: Is this blessedness only for the _____ (Jews), or also for the _____ (Gentiles)?

    o Romans 4:16: Therefore the _____ comes by faith, so that it may be by _____ and may be guaranteed to all Abraham's offspring—not only to those who are of the law (Jews), but also to those who are of the _____ of Abraham (Gentiles). He is the _____ of us all.

You, my friend, are part of God's fulfillment of His promise to Abraham. You are a spiritual child of Abraham. Will you build on Abraham's legacy of obedience to and faith in God as you live your life? God kept His promises to Abraham, and He will keep His promises to you.

MEDITATION MOMENT: Have you ever thought about being a spiritual child of Abraham? You are—if you are a believer in Jesus Christ. Thank God today for calling your heart into a saving relationship with Jesus. Pray for our Jewish brothers and sisters whose hearts have been hardened toward Christ. Ask God to open their eyes and hearts to the gospel.

Day 3—God's Promise to David

You're back! You worked hard yesterday, learning about God's promise to Abraham and how God ultimately fulfilled that promise in *you!* I hope you rewarded yourself with a bubble bath, a wonderful dessert, or a nice piece of chocolate. If you did not, feel free. You deserve it! Make sure you have another reward in mind, because today we will be busy as we examine the promises God made to David.

Let's continue perusing the Word of God to see God make a promise to David—and then fulfill that very promise. I hope you are beginning to see that God is the ultimate promise-keeper.

Go with me to 1 Chronicles 17 and read the entire chapter. It is only twenty-seven verses, so it won't take long. I'll be waiting for you to return.

Now that you have read 1 Chronicles 17, let's take it apart a bit and see God's promises to David—one whom God called a man after His own heart.

- What was David's desire?

- What was God's response from verse 4?

- In verse 8, we find the first promise that God made to David. What was it?

- The second promise, dealing with the nation of Israel, is found in verse 9. Note it here.

- Promise number three is found at the end of verse 10. Write it here.

- Verse 11 shifts the focus from Israel back to David's family. What promise does God make in verse 11?

- More promises—what promise do you find in verse 12?

- Verses 13 and 14 are *major!* What does this promise say?

Good work. Now, let's go back and see if we can discover the fulfillment of each of these promises.

There is little question that David was the greatest of the Israelite kings. He not only served as king, but was a warrior, poet, musician, shepherd, and ancestor of the Lord Jesus Christ. If you go to Jerusalem today, you can stay in the King David Hotel. When you open your Bible to the very center, you will likely be looking at one of the Psalms written by David. Yes, God most definitely kept His promise to make David's name great.

The second and third promises concern the nation of Israel. God promised to give them a home of their own so they would no longer be disturbed and oppressed. He also promised to subdue their enemies. The fulfillment of these promises is detailed in 1 Chronicles 18–20, where David's victories over the Philistines at Gath and the nations of Moab, Ammon, and Amalek allowed him to expand his kingdom so that he was known all throughout the world at that time.

The final promises, detailed in 1 Chronicles 17 verses 10–14 are where I would like us to camp for a while. In these verses, God promised David that instead of David building a house for God, God would build a house for David. It would not be a physical house made of stone and bricks, but rather a line of descendants who would forever rule and reign. Let's examine this lineage—this legacy that God gave David.

1 Chronicles 17:11 tells us that God promised to raise up one of David's offspring to succeed him as king.

- According to 1 Kings 2:10–12, who succeeded David as King?

- How was he related to King David?

- Glance at verse 13 and note the name of Solomon's mother.

God raised up Solomon, the son of Bathsheba, to become king of Israel after David died. Solomon, rather than David, was allowed to build a temple for the presence of God to dwell among the Israelites.

Take a look at the last part of 1 Chronicles 17:12. What does it say? "I will establish his throne forever." This promise is echoed in Jeremiah 33:17 where the prophet Jeremiah repeats Samuel's prophecy that says, "David will never fail to have a man to sit on the throne of the house of Israel." What is that about? We all know that there is not a king ruling in Israel today, nor has there been since the Israelites were carried off into captivity hundreds of years before Jesus was born.

Read verses 13–14 once again. These verses are telling us of an eternal promise that God made to David. Although David likely had no idea that this was an eternal promise and it would be fulfilled through the coming of the Messiah, this promise was ultimately fulfilled in Jesus Christ. Let's remind ourselves of this.

- In Luke 3:21–22, we find the story of John's baptism of Jesus. What does the voice from heaven proclaim about Jesus?

Hebrews 1 enlarges our understanding of this Father/Son relationship between God the Father and Jesus Christ, His Son. The writer of Hebrews is seeking to convince the Jews of his day that Jesus is greater than the angels, and the author does this by focusing on the fact that Jesus is the Son of God and no angel can ever lay claim to that relationship with God.

- Fill in the blanks from Hebrews 1:5: "For to which of the angels did _____ever say, 'You are my _____; today I have become your _____' or again, 'I will be his _____ and he will be my _____:'"

- Then the writer of Hebrews affirms the eternality of Jesus' kingship in verse 8 when he says about the Son, "Your throne, O God, will last for _____ and _____:"

In Jeremiah 33, we are given a powerful prophecy regarding the covenant—the promises—that God made to David. Go with me to Jeremiah 33:14–22 and read this passage slowly and thoughtfully, then answer the following questions:

- Who are the "house of Israel and the house of Judah" referred to in verse 14?

- Jeremiah talks about a "righteous branch" that sprouts from the line of David. To whom do you think he is referring?

In Jeremiah 33:19–22, God makes a very strong statement regarding the keeping of His promise to David. He says that His promise—His covenant with David—will only be broken if and when He breaks His promise to bring forth the day and the night at their appointed times. The last time I checked, the daytime and nighttime still arrive right on schedule! God is still keeping His promise to David.

One day, Jesus will return to this earth to set up the earthly kingdom that He did not have the first time He walked this earth. His kingdom will be eternal; there will be no end. This will be the ultimate fulfillment of God's promise to David. David's promise from God was a dual promise; part was fulfilled in the days of the ancient kings, and part will be fulfilled when Jesus comes back to earth to rule and reign.

God always keeps His promises. He just doesn't always promise that He will do it within our lifetime. When the generations that come behind you examine your legacy, will they see that you were faithful to God—even when you had to wait on His timing to see His promises to you fulfilled?

MEDITATION MOMENT: Can you think of a promise that has been made to you by God which has not currently been fulfilled? Are you willing to trust that God will keep His promise, even if it means the fulfillment will not come in your lifetime? Spend some time journaling your thoughts about this.

Day 4—God's Promises about Jesus

In his book *The Case For Christ,* Lee Strobel lays out a carefully researched argument for the existence of Jesus Christ. Strobel, a former atheist, was challenged to examine the claims concerning Jesus when his wife, Leslie, came to him telling him that she had become a Christian. An investigative journalist, Strobel decided to treat this information in the same manner that he would a breaking news story. He would interview the experts and do the research in order to find the most accurate and up-to-date information available concerning Jesus.

One of the experts whom Strobel interviewed was Louis S. Lapides, pastor of Beth Ariel Fellowship in Sherman Oaks, California. Lapides, a Jewish boy from Newark, New Jersey, holds a bachelor's degree in theology from Dallas Baptist University, a master of divinity, and a master of theology degree in Old Testament and Semitics from Talbot Theological Seminary. He has long worked with Jewish college students through Chosen People Ministries in an effort to lead them to Jesus. He also works with Walk Through the Bible Ministries.

How did this Jewish man come to faith in Christ? It was through his own examination of the prophecies, or promises, that God made concerning the Messiah. When challenged in 1969 by a pastor to examine the prophecies concerning a Jewish Messiah, Lapides exclaimed that he had never heard of the prophecies. The pastor encouraged him to take the Bible and read the Old Testament, asking "the God of Abraham, Isaac, and Jacob—the God of Israel—to show you if Jesus is the Messiah." [11]

Lapides began reading the Old Testament, seeing first one prophecy and then another. When he finished the Old Testament, he had read more than fifty prophecies about the Messiah. He knew that he needed to find out more. He then took a very drastic step for a good Jewish man. He decided to read the first page—only the first page—of the New Testament. He opened the book of Matthew and was stunned to read the geneology of "Jesus Christ, the son of David, the son of Abraham." Ultimately Lapides came to know Jesus as his Lord and Savior.

Throughout the Old Testament, God made over fifty promises concerning Jesus. Just as Louis Lapides came to know Jesus though the promises that God made and then kept, so we can draw closer to Him in faith by examining them. Let's get started.

- I am going to provide you with two references in the Bible for each promise—a reference for the prophecy, and then a reference for the fulfillment of that prophecy. Match the prophecy reference with the verse that tells of the fulfillment of that prophecy. On the line next to the fulfillment prophecy, note the details of prophecy and fulfillment. I'll do the first one for you.

Prophecy	Fulfillment	Details
Psalm 2:7	Mark 15:28	
Isaiah 7:14	Matthew 2:1	
Micah 5:2	Luke 24:6,31,34	
Zechariah 13:7	Luke 1:32,35	Jesus was the Son of God
Psalm 41:9;55:12-14	Mark 14:65	
Zechariah 11;13	Matthew 1:18,23	
Isaiah 50:6	Matthew 26:31, 56	
Psalm 22:16	John 13:18,21,25-27; 18:2-3	
Isaiah 53:12	John 19:18; 20:25	
Psalm 16:10	Matthew 26: 15-16	

Promise made—promise kept. God is all about keeping His promises, and when He promised a Messiah who would take away sin, He did exactly what He said He would do. He sent Jesus to live on this earth as a man, be persecuted, and be rejected by men. He died a horrible death on the cross to pay the fine for my sin and your sin, yet rose from the grave on the third day to bring not only forgiveness of sin, but life everlasting to you and to me.

You have worked so hard looking up promises today, and I'm so proud of you. There is one more prophecy that I want you to read. It comes from the prophet Isaiah, and is so beautiful that it brings tears to my eyes when I read it. Please don't skip over this. It is a stunning ending to our look at God's promises.

MEDITATION MOMENT: Before you turn to Isaiah 53, please pause and ask the Lord to give you fresh eyes and a heart that is tender toward His Word in this moment. Ask Him to help you picture Jesus as the suffering servant who came to take away your sin and give you His glory. Read Isaiah 53 carefully and prayerfully.

Day 5—What about Me?

This week, we have examined God's promises to Abraham and David. We also perused some of the promises that God made concerning Jesus and gazed at the fulfillment of those promises. Right about now, you may be asking yourself, "But what about me? Has God made any promises to me? And even more importantly, has He—or will He—keep whatever He promises to *me?*"

Those are very good questions. If God's promises are not pertinent to our lives, then all the work we have done this week is nothing more than a lesson in ancient history. So let's seek to make God's promises applicable to our lives today, in this very moment.

I want us to explore three of the promises that God made to us today, and as we do this, we will spend some time journaling about how God has been faithful to keep these promises in our lives.

Promise #1

- Please read John 14:16–18, 25–26 and note what Jesus promised to do.

- List the names by which the Holy Spirit is called in these verses.

- What did Jesus promise that the Holy Spirit would do for us?

Until Jesus' death and resurrection, the Holy Spirit had not permanently indwelt a human. He was sent by God to minister in and through various people, and we read about that in many places in the Bible. King David knew about this temporary ministry of the Holy Spirit, and He desired it in his life. In Psalm 51:10–12, we hear David begging the Lord to not remove the Spirit from him as a result of his sin with Bathsheba and the murder of Uriah. A plea this passionate could only come from one who had experienced the presence and power of the Holy Spirit.

Jesus promised to send the Spirit to lead, guide, counsel, and comfort the followers of Christ after his death and resurrection. The writer of the book of Acts, Dr. Luke, gives us a very detailed account of this promise coming to pass in chapters 1 and 2 of Acts.

Right about now, you should be asking, "So what about *me?* How does this relate *to me?*" Think back to the tasks that Jesus promised the Holy Spirit would accomplish. He said that the Holy Spirit would be a counselor, a guide to truth, a teacher, and a holy string around your finger to remind you of what God said.

In my own life, I have seen the Holy Spirit operate in all of these roles so many times. He guides me to truth as I study the Word of God and pray. He is a teacher to me, instilling God's wisdom in me as I open my heart and mind to receive it. He is a reminder to me of the sacrifice that Jesus made for me and the rewards that come from being His child. He also reminds me that He rescued me out of some major pits and potholes. This reminder keeps me focused on staying close to Christ so that I never return to those pits. Finally, the Holy Spirit has so often been my counselor and my guide as I seek to make decisions that are pleasing to God. He has also guided and counseled me through difficult seasons in my life through the wisdom of other people, Bible studies, and prayer.

- Now it is your turn. Choose one of the tasks of the Holy Spirit (counselor, teacher, guide, or reminder) and journal a bit about the ways that He has worked in your life in that particular role.

Promise #2

Former Surgeon General Dr. C. Everett Koop said, "We grow and mature spiritually through adversity—not when everything is going smoothly …. [I]n a time of adversity or trouble, the Christian has the opportunity to know God is a special and personal way."[12]

I have never met a single person who has prayed to have trouble and trials come into their lives just so they can grow and mature spiritually—not one! Think about it. We take vaccinations to avoid becoming sick. We exercise to ward off heart disease and diabetes. We diet to keep from being obese so that we do not experience the health problems that come as a result of obesity. We are mandated to wear seat belts to keep us safe. We participate in pre-marital counseling in hopes of avoiding difficulties in marriage. Let's face it. We are all about living the easy life, and most people don't want to work too hard to have it.

- In John 16:33, Jesus sticks a holy pin in our human bubble. Complete Jesus' words to us about trials and difficulties. "I have told you these things so that in me you may have _____. In this world you _____ have _____. But take heart! I have overcome the _____ _____."

Not exactly what we want to hear, is it? As long as we live in this world, we are going to have difficulties, troubles, and trials. It is a fact of life. Read the newspaper, listen to the news, read your church's prayer list. Troubles and trials are no respecter of persons. They affect the young and the old, the rich and the poor, the tall and the short, women and men—everyone. This brings us to one of the promises that God made to us.

- Read Isaiah 43:1–2 and note what promise God made to us.

God promised that He would be with us as we go through troubles and trials. He would not allow us to go through them alone. Notice in this verse that God did not say, *"if* you pass through or walk through trials."* He said *"when* we go through troubles and trials," He will be there with us.

So often, when we experience trouble, we determine in our hearts that we will pull ourselves up by the bootstraps and deal with our problems on our own. That, my friend, is pride. When we do that, we are telling God to get lost; we don't need His help. What a slap in the face of the God who has promised to be there with us in our difficulties! Only God has the solution for all our problems. Only He is able to bring us through in victory.

Sometimes we are so paralyzed by fear of a situation that we fail to seek God's help in the middle of our dark night. God longs to speak into our fear and provide His help.

- In the following verses, God tell us "do not fear" several times. Note what God promises to us even as He tells us not to fear:

  o   Isaiah 41:10

  o   Isaiah 41:13

Do not fear! Do not fear when you pass through the waters and through the rivers. Do fear when you walk through the fire. God will be with you, holding your right hand with His own righteous right hand.

Picture God taking you by your right hand using His own right hand. In order for one person to take another by the right hand, that person has to be facing the one whose hand he is taking. God takes our right hand with His own and looks us straight in the eye and says, "Do not fear." God doesn't walk behind us holding our hand, nor does He walk beside us. He walks in front of us and is so completely in control of our circumstances that He even walks backward, holding our hand, looking straight into our eyes. He says, "I'm here, just keep your eyes on My eyes and let Me lead you."

- Once again, it is your turn to journal about a time in your life when you were in the middle of trouble or a trial, yet sensed the presence of the Lord with you. Perhaps your journaling may be about a time when you only recognized God's presence with you after you came out of a trial.

Promise #3

The final promise that I want us to look at today is one that we will have to claim by faith until we breathe our last of this earthly air.

- What two things does Jesus promise to you and to me in John 14:1–3?

It will only be when this veil of flesh falls away that we will be able to dwell in the fulfillment of this promise of Jesus—a promise to prepare a place for us in heaven and to one day take us to live with Him. Although there are fleeting moments of peace and joy in this life, we will experience unending peace and overflowing joy when we dwell in the presence of Jesus Christ in heaven. There will be no more fear, anxiety, depression, tears, or disease. Our best day on earth will not even begin to resemble anything that heaven holds for us. We will live in the presence of the One who gave His very life for us. We are His inheritance, and He is ours.

I hope that you have come to truly understand that God keeps His promises. He always has, and He always will. He is exactly who He says He is, and He is worthy of our faith and trust. As we trust God in faith and find Him faithful in the small trials in our lives, then we will be able to trust Him in faith as larger trials are allowed by Him in our lives. It is a cycle. The more we trust Him, the more we find Him faithful; the more we find Him faithful, the more we trust Him—and on and on it goes. Faith—the first building block of a godly legacy that we leave for those who come behind us.

MEDITATION MOMENT: How is your faith? Is it strong and vibrant? Or could it use a boost? Ask God to increase your faith in Him. That is a prayer that He will definitely answer.

Week 4—When Character Was King

The great civil rights leader, Dr. Martin Luther King, Jr., spoke very wise words when he said, "We must be judged not by the color of our skin but the content of our character."[13]

Character. According to the Encarta Dictionary, *character* is defined as "the set of qualities that make somebody or something distinctive, especially somebody's qualities of mind and feeling."[14] I would argue that godly character is so much more. It is a set of qualities instilled by God into a person that causes them to be distinctive—to stand out in a world that is more interested in reputation than character.

This week, as we continue our quest to build a godly legacy for the generations that come behind us, we will reflect on this issue of character. There are many elements of a godly legacy, and we will look at just a few of them, hoping that what we find will move us to thoughtfully consider how our character measures up to God's standard.

Week 4 Goals:

- Identify what a woman of noble character looks like

- Think through the implications of sins such as lying, gossip, and a lack of trustworthiness

Day 1—A 5:22 Picture of Character

In 2006, I went with a group from my church on a fifteen-day trip to the Israel and Egypt. Going to Israel and seeing the land where Jesus walked was truly the trip of a lifetime. I will never study the Bible in quite the same way after experiencing the land, because now I see in my mind the places about which the Bible speaks. In Israel I walked through the Garden of Gethsemane and stood on the Mount of Olives facing the eastern gate of the old temple compound. I had the opportunity to stand at the Western Wall and place a thoughtfully constructed prayer into the crevices. I stood in awe inside the tomb where Jesus was buried and worshipped our risen Lord in the garden outside the tomb. Truly, my faith was deepened by my experiences in the land of Israel, and I hope to return one day.

One of the places that we visited in Jerusalem was the pool of Siloam where crews were doing an archaeological dig, looking for treasures from the temple era. As the men dumped buckets of dirt into a sieve, water was run over the contents of the buckets and the dirt was washed away, leaving only stones and artifacts in the basket of the sieve. Anything of value was immediately taken away, while everything else was taken to a dumpster located just outside the area of the dig and discarded.

As we left the pool area, we happened upon the dumpster, and one lady in our group saw something that appeared to be a piece of broken pottery. It turned out to be a piece off the handle of a tea pot or other jug. We were like sharks at a crappie convention. Immediately our entire group—men and women alike—were digging through the dumpster contents to find anything that even remotely resembled an ancient treasure. Even the most refined among us lowered themselves to dumpster diving at that moment—and in fact, a few people brought home nice-sized pieces of broken pottery.

All too often in our current culture, we stoop to dumpster diving when it comes to our character rather than seeking out those true treasures that build character and a godly legacy—true treasures like honesty; trustworthiness; and refraining from gossip, backbiting, and slander that only shine forth as we seek to allow God to work in and through us.

The word *character* is used three times in the Old Testament, and each time, the word *character* is combined with the word *noble.* Noble character. There is a common theme running through each of these three verses.

- Look up each of the following verses and note the common denominator in each: Ruth 3:11, Proverbs 12:4, and Proverbs 31:10.

Did you find the common denominator? Each time the word character is used, it is in reference to a woman. Each of these verses highlights the issue of the character of a woman and what a valuable asset a woman of noble character is to a man. Before someone goes feminist and writes me a long letter about how women are not possessions of men, please understand that I do not mean valuable asset in terms of a possession. Rather, it appears that the Word of God is telling us that a woman of noble character makes her man look better, and he is darned lucky to have her.

Today I want us to turn our attention to a passage of scripture that paints a picture in primary colors of a woman of godly character. This passage does not speak specifically of women, but once you read it, I think you will understand my goal in having you study this passage.

- Read Galatians 5:22 and make a list of the things that would be painted into our picture of a woman of godly character.

Picture in your mind a woman you know who exhibits each of the fruits of the Spirit as we walk through them briefly.

Love. Love for all, regardless of who they are, where they live, or what they smell like. True love is not conditional. Jesus' love for you and for me was not conditional on our ability to clean ourselves up before we came to Him. He loved us long before we ever loved Him. That is the Spirit's love, and we are called to love others in the same way.

Joy. Notice this verse does not say *happiness.* Happiness is dependent on external circumstances, while joy comes from within and can be present even in the midst of trial and trouble. True joy comes from Jesus and knowing that He is living in and walking with you. True joy can be present even in the midst of trouble and trial.

Peace. Oh, how our world longs for and needs peace! Yet peace does not come from the world.

- What did Jesus say about peace in John 14:27?

Peace can only be found by having Jesus living in your heart.

Patience. In the New Testament, there are two words used for patience. The first is *makrothymia,* used in this verse to describe the fruit of the Spirit. This word means "self-restraint before proceeding to action. The quality of a person who has power to avenge himself, yet refrains from doing so."[15] This word describes a patience with regard to people ,and this is a quality that you and I desperately need to acquire. Jesus was the ultimate example of *makrothymia,* exhibiting patience with those around Him in remarkable ways. Most notably, His patience with his twelve closest companions, the disciples, offers endless study in the concept of *makrothymia.*

Another word use interchangeably for *patience is perseverance.* The Greek word for perseverance is *hypomone,* and it means "to bear up under, remain under." Listen to the rest of the definition: "Hypomone is associated with hope and refers to that quality of character that does not allow one to surrender to circumstances or succumb under trial."[16]

- We find this word, *perseverance,* used in Romans 5:3–4. Fill in the blanks and see the relationship between character and patience or perseverance.

  "We also rejoice in our sufferings, because we know that suffering produces _____ _____; perseverance produces _____; and character, _____."

Patience produces character, and character produces hope! Now there's a reason to work on having a godly character! We all need hope!

Kindness and goodness. We live in a world devoid of kindness and goodness; therefore, those who are truly kind and good stand out like sore thumbs. This kindness and goodness should flow from having Jesus in your heart. His desires and actions are good, and when He lives in us, our hearts should reflect Christ's desires and actions.

Faithfulness. Commitment. Staying the course, even when it is hard. Jesus is the ultimate example for us of faithfulness. He did the hard thing. He died on the cross and took our punishment so that we could stand clean before a holy God.

- In Hebrews 12:2, we are told that Jesus was faithful to endure the cross for what reason? What was the joy set before Him?

Jesus was looking forward to the time when He would be reunited with the Father. Knowing that one day, we who are Christians will be together with Jesus in heaven is the reason for you and me to stay faithful to run the race in this life.

Gentleness. Our world is not gentle. It is rough, and it expects us to be the same. As women seeking to leave a godly legacy, we must exhibit a gentleness of spirit and heart, an inward grace of the soul that will be attractive to those desperately needing a haven from the toughness of the world.

Self-control. "Anything goes! If it feels good, do it!" As the moral compass of our nation and world has spun crazily away from True North, the concept of self-control seems to have gone the way of the dinosaur.

This issue of self-control is crucial when we are making moral decisions. Charles Allen offers four questions to ask when making moral decisions, and at the core of each is the issue of self-control. Ponder these questions:

1. Would you need to keep it a secret?

2. Where will it lead you?

3. Which is your best self?

4. What would the person you admire the most do if he/she were in your situation?[17]

These are powerful questions to consider when making moral decisions that will affect your character, my friend. As we go through this week of study and contemplate our character, I urge you to make an effort to honestly evaluate yourself in light of what we are studying.

I want us to take a moment to consider those people in our lives who have left us a legacy of faith, character, and holiness. For most of us, as we consider those important people in our lives, we recognize that we are often drawn to them because of one of the fruits of the Spirit. Personally, I remember a precious woman in the church where I grew up who was the epitome of gentleness. Her name was Verna Hamilton, and I remember as a child thinking that she must be the most gentle and kind person I had ever met. Although she has been with Jesus for many years now, my memories of her gentle and quiet spirit are part of the legacy that she left for those who came behind her.

*   In the margin, write the names of three people who have impacted your life in a positive way and share which of the fruits of the Spirit you saw evidenced in their lives.

MEDITATION MOMENT: Consider Galatians 5:22 from *The Message:* "But what happens when we live God's way? He brings gifts into our lives, much the same way that fruit appears in an orchard—things like affection for others, exuberance about life, serenity. We develop a willingness to stick with things, a sense of compassion in the heart, and a conviction that a base holiness permeates things and people. We find ourselves involved in loyal commitments, not needing to force our way in life, able to marshal and direct our energies wisely."[18] Ask the Spirit to reveal to you which of these fruits are lacking in your life. Spend some time journaling about what He shows you.

Day 2—The Gossip Girls

In the late 1960s and early 1970s, the television program *Hee Haw* was required viewing on Saturday nights at my grandparents' home. My sister, Leslie, and I would often spend the night with my grandparents on Saturday nights, and after supper, the television—which received only three channels—would be tuned to the one that broadcast *Hee Haw*. One of the feature skits on *Hee Haw* was "The Gossip Girls," and each week they indulged in a bit of gossip about one of the other characters on the show. Do you remember the song they sang?

> Now, we're not ones to go 'round spreadin' rumors
>
> Why, really we're just not the gossipy kind
>
> No, you'll never hear one of us repeating gossip
>
> So you'd better be sure and listen close the first time! [19]

No, they were not going to be accused of *repeating* gossip, but they sure were not shy about sharing it the first time.

Gossip is defined as "conversation about the personal details of the lives of other people." The conversation could be either rumor or truth. When gossip turns malicious and cruel with the intent to harm, it becomes slander.

Unfortunately, women seem to be particularly adept at gossip, slander, and backbiting, and the Bible has a great deal to say about this sin. Yes, you read that correctly. It is sin, and it displeases God greatly.

Before some of you mentally check out on me, thinking that this topic does not apply to you, please consider whether or not you have ever shared a "prayer request" with another person, knowing very well that the request really did not need to be shared. You only shared that prayer request because you want to pass along information and perhaps be the *first* to get the word out that poor Betty is going through such a rough time. If someone shares a prayer request with you and does not specifically say to pass it on, *don't!* God knows the need of the person, and He does not need your help in making sure the right people are praying. A personal prayer request belongs to the person who voiced it, and it is not your responsibility or mine to spread it abroad. I dare say that we have all been guilty of this form of gossip, so stick with me here.

Winston Churchill knew about gossip and backbiting.

> He was attending an official ceremony in London. Two men behind him recognized him and began to whisper behind his back.
>
> "They say Churchill's quite senile now," said the one.
>
> "Yes, they say he's doing England more harm than good," replied the other.
>
> "They say he should step aside and leave the running of this government to younger, more dynamic people," continued the first man.
>
> Churchill turned and in a loud voice said, "They also say he's quite deaf."[20]

King David knew about the damage caused by gossip, backbiting, and slander. In Psalm 57:4, he openly talks about the people who are attacking him when he says, "I am in the midst of lions; I lie among ravenous beasts—men whose teeth are spears and arrows, whose tongues are sharp swords."

I want us to take some time and examine what God's Word says about this issue of using our tongues as sharp swords for the purpose of gossip and backbiting.

First, let us consider that God takes this business of the sin of the tongue very seriously. Fill in the blanks in the following verses from the Old Testament:

- Psalm 50:19–21: "You use your mouth for _____ and harness your tongue to _____. You speak continually ___ _____ your brother and _____ your own mother's son. These things _____have done and I kept silent; you thought I was altogether _____ _____. But I will rebuke you and _____ you to your face."

- Proverbs 10:18: "Whoever spreads slander is a _____."

God is crystal clear regarding how he feels about slander and deceitful tongues, isn't He? We are badly mistaken if we think that He will turn His head and ignore our gossip and backbiting.

Second, God warns against the sin of gossip, backbiting, and slander through the pen of the apostle Paul. In the New Testament, as in the Old, God minces no words about gossip and slander.

- In 2 Timothy 3:1–5, Paul warns of terrible times in the last days before Jesus returns to this earth. List some of the signs of those times. Be sure to notice that slanderous people are included in this list.

- What command did Paul give in the end of verse 5 about the type of people who would be present in the last days?

Paul urged the Christians in Galatia to have nothing to do with people who are slanderous. Pretty strong words, huh? That is how seriously God takes these sins of the tongue. He knows the potential damage that is encompassed in our tongues, and He wants His children to steer clear of the people who engage in such evil.

Unfortunately, this has become one of the more accepted sins in the Christian community today. While we seek to condemn a person who commits murder, we choose to turn our heads when one Christian gossips about or slanders another. We must understand that God does not view sin in degrees. Sin is sin—period. It is all an affront to a holy God, and He will tolerate none of it. While we sit about our kitchen tables sharing coffee and gossip and rationalize that we are not as bad as someone who has an affair or commits murder, God looks down and shakes His head at us because we allow Satan to deceive us about our sin.

In the classic passage on women mentoring other women, Paul advises Titus to teach right living to his congregation.

- In Titus 2:3–5, Paul charges the older women with some very important tasks. What are they?

Ladies, if you have been walking with Christ for more than a few weeks, you might be considered an older woman to someone who is just coming to know Jesus as Lord. Someone is always inspecting our lives. Those who hear us profess to be a Christian but also hear us spread gossip or slander our brothers and sisters will wonder what makes a Christian different from any other religious person.

Finally, listen to the words of Charles Swindoll about this topic of gossiping: "We live in a day of hearsay, when few people pass along information that is precise and reliable. Do you? Are you careful about what you say? Do you have the facts? Do you offer proof that the information you are conveying is correct? While there are occasions when it's appropriate to pass along needed and serious information to the right sources, there's a growing preoccupation with rumor and slander. Half-truths and innuendos become juicy morsels in the mouths of unreliable gossips. There is no way to measure the number of people who have been hurt by rumor, exaggeration, and hearsay. Perhaps you have suffered this yourself …. Be careful what you say. Be careful how you say it. Be careful that you send the right message, that you send it to the right person, and that you do so with the right motive." [21]

Today, my friends, is when we find out if we are really serious about living a life that leaves a godly legacy. God is turning up the heat as we seek to walk in the footsteps of Christ and look more like Him. I'm going to ask you to take a bold step today as we think about this issue of gossip, backbiting, and slander.

Instead of looking up more Scriptures on this topic, I want us to look into our hearts and allow the Holy Spirit to expose any tendencies toward gossip or backbiting that exist. In order to do this, please identify two people you would consider to be friends who will tell you the truth, rather than telling you what they think you want to hear. Schedule a time to telephone or sit down with these two friends separately. Explain to them that you are doing a Bible study which calls you to examine your character and ask them to tell you honestly if you are considered to be a person who engages in gossip, backbiting, or slander. These people need to be able to be completely honest with you, without fear of anger or reprisal from you.

Most of us will probably hear answers that we do not like, because most of us engage in gossip and backbiting. My goal in this exercise is not to cause hurt feeling between friends, but rather to do a bit of shock therapy in order to stun us into seeing ourselves and our actions for what they truly are—a sin against God.

Once you talk with your friends, spend some time talking with God about what you learned. Allow Him to reveal any tendencies toward gossip, backbiting, and slander in your heart and life. Ask Him to help you to be aware of when you are doing those things and to stop them. Request forgiveness for specific instances that the Holy Spirit brings to your mind. Ask Him to enable you to seek forgiveness from those you have hurt with gossip, backbiting, and slander.

Girl, you have done some incredibly hard work today. I know it has not been easy, but the payoffs are huge. As you seek to keep your words pleasing to God, He will reward those efforts in ways that you cannot even imagine. Do *not* allow Satan to bring shame and condemnation into your mind over anything the Holy Spirit has revealed today. Walk ahead in the knowledge that your heavenly Father loves you more than you can possibly imagine. Be assured that He esteems the hard work you are doing so that you can leave a godly legacy for those who come behind.

MEDITATION MOMENT: Write a prayer of thanksgiving to God for His faithful, unconditional love and forgiveness toward you.

Day 3—May the Words of My Mouth ...

I have always been a fairly outspoken person, often to my own detriment—and most certainly to the detriment of others. All too often when my mouth opened, whatever was on my mind came out of it—and it was not always said in love.

Several years after Greg and I married, I began to learn that my husband would be a person in my life who would tell me the things I needed to hear, regardless of how angry it made me. He does it because he loves me, although sometimes I don't feel the love in his words because it feels like I am being criticized and condemned. I am so thankful for Greg's wise counsel and guidance in my life.

One day, Greg and I were having one of those lively marital discussions better known as a disagreement. In the course of the discussion, Greg told me that I needed to think about the things I say, because often they are hurtful to others. When I asked for an example, he told me that there were many, but that he was not going into specifics. While that frustrated the stew out of me, it also caused me to begin thinking about the words I say to others and how even though I may not intend for them to be hurtful, often they are.

Another thing that my husband has made me aware of is my tendency to offer unsolicited opinions. Without even realizing it, I was interjecting my advice and opinions into conversations where they had not been requested. How rude!

As I have sought to walk closer with the Lord and hide His Word in my heart, I am slowly retraining myself to guard my tongue and allow it to speak more words of kindness and graciousness and fewer words of condemnation and harshness.

God's Word has much to say about our tongue, and I want us to take time today to mine these truths and allow the Holy Spirit to implant them deep in our heart. Much of our time together today will be spent in the Word—so grab your Bible, and let's get started.

First, let's return to the passage where we began our week of study. In Galatians 5:22, we are told that the fruit that is produced from having the presence of Christ and His Spirit within our hearts includes love, joy, peace, patience, kindness, goodness, gentleness, faithfulness, and self-control.

- How many of these fruits pertain either directly or indirectly to the tongue and the words that we say?

If you said "all of them," you are right. The presence or absence of every single one of these fruit can show up in the words we speak.

- What did the psalmist proclaim in the final sentence of Psalm 17:3?

If we are going to speak words of kindness and graciousness to others, we must resolve that our mouths will not sin. We must give control of our tongues over to Jesus and purpose in our hearts to allow our words to be ones that would honor God. How do we do this?

- What does Proverbs 2:6 tell us comes from the Lord?

- In Proverbs 4:5, 7, we are told to get something. What should we get, even if it costs us all we have?

If we get wisdom and understanding from God, then we will have the discernment that we need to use our tongues in ways that honor God and bless others.

Let's examine a few more verses that deal with our tongues. Note what each verse says about our tongues and our speech"

- Proverbs 4:24

- Proverbs 10:13

- Proverbs 10:21

- Proverbs 11:9

- Proverbs 13:3

- Proverbs 16:24

- Proverbs 17:28

- Proverbs 18:2

- Proverbs 21:23

- Proverbs 25:11

Do you see the need to allow the Holy Spirit to hold the reigns of our tongue in order to create a godly legacy? Can you identify problem areas in your life with regard to your tongue? What do you believe Jesus would have you do to correct those problem areas? Only by allowing Jesus to control our mouths will we speak words that are kind and gracious to others. There is a medieval proverb that says, "If a man's life be lightning, his words are thunder." Let us allow Jesus to make our words like a gentle thunder to the ears of others.

MEDITATION MOMENT: Close your time in the Word by praying Psalm 19:14.

Day 4—Liar, Liar, Pants on Fire

I despise for someone to lie to me. I believe that I would prefer they steal from me than lie to me. I hate lying, yet it has become one of the most accepted and dumbed-down sins of our day. I read some statistics many years ago that said greater than 90% of Americans admit they lie on a regular basis. Did you get that? Greater than 90%. Nine out of every ten people you meet will admit to lying on a regular basis. Do you? It is an issue that I was confronted with personally, because sometimes the Lord uses that which we hate most to refine us.

One spring day a few years ago, I had promised my young nephew that I would come to his baseball game. My sister told me that the game would be starting at 7:00 pm, which is late for me. I am one of those early-to-bed, early-to-rise folks, and by 7:00 pm I am beginning to wind down for the evening.

However, I had promised Parker I would come to his game, and so I went. Halfway through the game, I decided that probably Parker was so engrossed in his game that he would never notice if I slipped out. After all, I'm not the mom; I'm the aunt. So I packed up my chair and began to make my way out of the crowd. I had to pass the dugout where Parker and his teammates were waiting to bat, and I tried to walk behind some other people and keep my exit hidden from Parker.

I was almost past the dugout when I heard Parker yell, "Aunt Leah, where you going?"

I walked over to the dugout, looked directly at Parker and said, "Uncle Greg is waiting on me at home to fix his supper. I need to go. You are playing great. Keep it up. I love you."

Parker said, "Okay. See ya," and turned his attention to his ballgame.

Before I could get to my car, a wave of guilt washed over me that threatened to completely engulf me. My husband was at a meeting that night which included a meal. I would not even go near the kitchen when I went home. I had just lied to my nephew in order to justify leaving his game. I was crushed at what I had done. What kind of an example was I? The Holy Spirit convicted me so deeply that I cried all the way home. Satan put his two cents worth into the mix as well. He tried to convince me that Parker would never know that I had lied to him. I reminded Satan that it didn't matter whether Parker ever knew or not. I knew, and I could not live with knowing that I had lied to him. I had to set a positive example of humility and repentance for my nephew.

Once home, I got down on my knees and asked the Lord to forgive me for lying to Parker. He did, but He also said, "Now, you have to confess what you did to Parker." I said, "Yes, Lord, I do."

The next day, I asked my sister to bring Parker to my house after school. I took him aside and said to him, "Parker, do you remember me telling you that the reason I had to leave your game last night was because I had to go home and fix Uncle Greg's dinner?"

Parker said, "Yes."

"I lied to you about the reason I left your ballgame early, Parker," I confessed, with tears flowing down my face. "Uncle Greg was at a meeting, and I did not have to fix his supper. I was just tired and wanted to go home. I am sorry that I lied to you. It was wrong of me, and I hope you will forgive me."

"That's okay, Aunt Leah," Parker replied.

Wanting to make sure he understood the gravity of my sin, I said to him, "No, Parker, it isn't okay. It is never okay to tell a lie. Never. Please forgive me."

"I do, Aunt Leah."

I had done the very thing that I hate. How in the world could that have happened? Let's examine what happened. I truly believe that as we seek to become more like Jesus, the Holy Spirit will turn up the heat on us, bringing the impurities in our hearts to the surface so they can be dealt with and discarded. Almost daily, I pray for the Lord to reveal any sin in my heart. That is exactly what He did. He reminded me that my heart is deceitfully wicked and that if I do not stay in close relationship with Him, I will slide into a pit of sin almost without even knowing what is happening.

Study after study confirms that lying is on the increase in America. One online survey of almost 7,000 persons performed by the Josephson Institute of Ethics found that dishonesty of a high school student was often a predictor of adult behavior.[22] Listen to one chilling statistic from this survey. In this study, teens seventeen years of age and younger are five times more likely than those over the age of fifty to believe that lying and cheating are a necessary part of success.

In a study published in the September 2009 issue of the *Journal of Moral Education,* researchers found that parents lie to children surprisingly often in order "to either shape their behavior or make the child happy." These findings held true even in "parents who most strongly promoted the importance of honesty with their children." One of the researchers involved in this study stated that "regardless of whether parental lying is justified, parents should figure out their policy on it ahead of time."[23]

I know of one Parent who has figured out His policy on lying. Let's look at how God feels about lying.

- In Proverbs 6:16–19, we are told that there are six things the Lord hates and seven that are detestable to Him. List them in the margin.

Did you hear the strong language in those verses? God hates lying. It is detestable to him. God hates lying so much that it is mentioned twice in these verses.

In his book *Just Like Jesus,* author Max Lucado says something that each of us should consider before we tell a lie. Take this in. "Are you in a dilemma, wondering if you should tell the truth or not? The question to ask in such moments is 'Will God bless my deceit? Will He, who hates lies, bless a strategy built on lies? Will the Lord who loves truth bless the business of falsehoods? Will God honor the career of the manipulator?' … I don't think so either."[24]

Let's turn once more to the book of Proverbs and attempt to gain God's perspective on this important issue of lying and our character. Match the verse from Proverbs with what it tells us about lying.

A. Proverbs 12:17   _____One who pours out lies will perish.

B. Proverbs 12:22   _____A liar hates the person to whom she lies.

C. Proverbs 14:25   _____A false witness tells lies.

D. Proverbs 19:5   _____God hates dishonesty in business.

E. Proverbs 20:23   _____Honest answers are as pleasant as a kiss.

F. Proverbs 21:6   _____God hates lying lips.

G. Proverbs 24:26   _____A false witness is deceitful.

H. Proverbs 26:28   _____Riches acquired by lying will vanish and be troublesome.

God will not bless a person who lies. Unlike you and me, God does not view lying in degrees of severity. There are no "little white lies" to God. A lie is a lie, and God hates—even detests—them all.

If you and I are seeking to establish a godly legacy for those who come behind, we must deal with the issue of lying in our lives and hearts. It will only be when we ask God to expose the sin of lying in our lives and help us to turn from it that we will begin to have a character like that of Jesus Christ. Let us say with the writer of Proverbs, "Keep falsehood and lies far from me."

MEDITATION MOMENT: Very few of us are totally honest 100% of the time. Spend some time in prayer today asking the Lord to reveal any areas of dishonesty in your life and to break your heart over them. Also ask Him to quicken your spirit so that when you do tell a lie, you immediately recognize it and ask His forgiveness for it.

Day 5—Standing By Your Word

In his marvelous book entitled *Lessons from a Father to His Son,* former Senator and Attorney General of the United States John Ashcroft tells the story of Michael Jordon and his determination to be a man of character and trustworthiness before his family and the world.

Until 1997, Michael Jordan, indisputably the leading player in the NBA for over a decade, was never the highest paid player. When asked why he did not do what so many other players do—hold out on their contracts until they get more money—Michael replied, "I have always honored my word. I went for security. I had six-year contracts, and I always honored them. People said I was underpaid, but when I signed on the dotted line, I gave my word."

> Three years later, after several highly visible players reneged on their contracts, a reporter asked Michael once again about being underpaid, and he explained that if his kids saw their dad breaking a promise, how could he continue training them to keep their word?
>
> By not asking for a contract renegotiation, Michael Jordan spoke volumes to his children. He told them, "You stand by your word, even when that might go against you." His silence became a roar.[25]

Are you known as a person who stands by their word? Are you trustworthy and dependable? If you promise to do something, do you follow through faithfully? If someone tells you something in confidence, do you keep that confidence? Do you consistently give your employer a good day of work for a good day of pay? If you and I are seeking to be people of character, we must be trustworthy in the eyes of the world.

In Matthew 25:14–30, we find a story that reminds us of the necessity of being trustworthy. Read this passage now.

I want to put this parable into a modern-day context to help us understand it better. Let's assume that the king in this story is actually a businesswoman who owns many clothing stores. She decides to go away for several years and entrusts the clothing stores to three of her store managers. The first manager is allotted ten stores, and she works hard to make those stores as profitable as possible—offering high quality merchandise, good prices, excellent customer service, and periodic deep discount sales. By the time the businesswoman returns, the ten stores that this manager has been responsible for have doubled their profit.

A second manager was entrusted with five stores, and she worked hard, producing the same kind of results as the first manager. When the businesswoman returned, the five stores that had been entrusted to the second manager had also doubled their profit.

A third manager was entrusted with one store. This manager was fearful of making bad decisions and taking risks, so she closed the doors of the store so that she would not lose any of the businesswoman's money. When the businesswoman returned, the store that had been entrusted to the third manager still had the same merchandise in it, but no employees, because they had left to take other jobs. The businesswoman was exceedingly disappointed and very angry with the third manager and fired her on the spot, giving her store to the manager who had done well with the ten stores.

- Fill in the blanks from Matthew 25:29: "For everyone who has will be _____ _____ and he will have an abundance. Whoever does not have, even what he has will be taken away from him."

In this parable, Jesus makes the point that being faithful to do what you have been asked to do—what you have committed to do—speaks volumes about your character. This is true in every aspect of your life. Let's take a moment and think through some scenarios where being trustworthy and true to your word is crucial.

Marriage—You promised to love your spouse, in good times and bad, forsaking *all* others. Keep your word!

Job—You were hired to perform specific duties. You agreed to do those duties, and you are accepting a paycheck for doing those duties. Keep your word!

Volunteer Positions—You volunteered to keep the nursery at church or staff a booth at a charity event. Show up! Keep your word!

Confidential Information—Your friend or co-worker tells you something personal about her life and asks you not to repeat it. You promise that you will tell no one. Keep your word!

Friendships—You and a friend agreed to attend a function together, but now you have the opportunity to do something that is more fun. Keep your word!

Time—You know that a particular class or event begins at a certain time, and others are counting on you to be there. Keep your word!

- Okay, now it is your turn. Describe a scenario when you made a promise to do something and you failed to follow through on what you had promised—you were not trustworthy.

- Now describe a time when you made a promise to do something, and even through it was hard, you kept your word and did it.

God has some definite ideas about being trustworthy and being a person who follows through on our commitments. Read the following scriptures and note what they say about being trustworthy:

- Exodus 18:21—What did God instruct Moses to do with the trustworthy men whom he selected?

- Proverbs 11:13—What can a man (or woman) who is trustworthy be counted upon to do?

- Proverbs 31:10–12—A trustworthy wife brings a husband good rather than what?

- Daniel 6:4—Because of Daniel's trustworthiness, the other officials were unable to do what?

- Luke 16:11—If we expect God to bless us with the true riches of His kingdom, what do we have to be trustworthy with here on earth?

In 2 Corinthians 7:16, the apostle Paul makes a statement about the believers in Corinth that each of us should desire to be made about us. He says that he is glad that he can have complete confidence in the Corinthian believers. This is one verse where the King James Version gives a bit more emphasis when it says, "I rejoice therefore that I have confidence in you in all things." Paul knew that these Corinthian believers said what they meant and meant what they said. Their yes was yes, and their no was no. They followed through on their promises and were faithful to their word.

Okay, my friend, it is time for a bit of self-inspection with regard to this topic of trustworthiness. If you and I truly desire to have a character that leaves a godly legacy for the generations that come behind, we must be willing to ask ourselves the tough questions and then make necessary adjustments in our lives as they are revealed.

I would like to ask you to stop for a moment and ask the Lord to help you examine your life honestly as you think through the following questions for our Meditation Moment. If the Holy Spirit shows you an area of your life that needs some work, take the time to pray and ask Him to help you make the necessary changes. Write down what the Lord reveals to you, and consider asking someone who is close to you to help you be accountable to work on what the Lord shows you.

MEDITATION MOMENT: Consider the following questions:

1. If someone tells me something in confidence, do I keep that confidence—no matter how tempting it may be to tell another person?

2. Do I perform the tasks at my workplace or at school that my employer or teacher expects me to accomplish?

3. Am I loyal to my employer?

4. Have I taken anything from my workplace or elsewhere that is not mine to take—pens, notepads, paperclips, staples, money, time on the internet/e-mail, extra time during lunch or breaks, etc.?

5. When I am expected to be at a particular place at a specified time, am I on time or even a bit early?

6. If I volunteer for a position at church or in a civic organization, do I follow through and perform the tasks that I agreed to do?

7. If I am married, am I completely faithful to my spouse and my marriage covenant?

8. If I am married, do I show my spouse respect, both in public and in private?

9. Am I loyal to my friends?

Week 5—The Pursuit of Holiness

Holiness can seem to be elusive—and at times, impossible to grasp—for those of us who follow Christ. Although we are commanded to be holy, all too often we do not have the first clue how to obtain that holiness. This week, we will delve into this command to be holy and allow the Spirit of God to enlighten our hearts and minds regarding this issue of holiness.

Let me warn you—this week of work may be tough, because we will look into the areas of our lives where we often put up a "No Trespassing" sign to the Lord. Prepare to allow Him full access to your heart so that He can do the work that will bring about an increase in your holiness.

Week 5 Goals:

- Understand the meaning of holiness and how this word pertains to your life

- Identify areas of unholiness in your life that need to be changed

- Acknowledge the importance of modesty in dress in living a holy life

- Realize the importance of making a decision to not place yourself in situations that might give the appearance of compromise with the world's values

Day 1—What Do I Know of Holy?

Holy. Holiness. These are very spiritual, churchy-sounding words that Christians toss around freely, yet I'm not certain we really understand the meaning of them. I believe that if we truly understood the nuances of the word *holy,* we might not be so quick to use it. The pursuit of holiness is not for the faint of heart or the easy-street Christian. Yet if we desire to leave a godly legacy for the generations that come behind us, we will take the issue of our holiness very seriously.

Let's begin our day of study by tightening our belts around the definition of the word *holy.* In the Old Testament, the Hebrew word for holy, *qadash,* is used 172 times. *Qadash* means "to be clean, holy, to dedicate, sanctify, appointed."[26] Something that is considered holy is understood to be for the Lord's purpose and is kept clean and pure in a unique way.

- Turn to the following scriptures and describe the things that were considered to be *qadash,* or holy. Note that the word *holy* may not be used in these passages. Instead you may find the words *consecrated* or *sanctified.*

  o Genesis 2:3

  o Exodus 29:36

  o Joshua 7:13

From these verses, you can hopefully see that the word *holy* can be applied to almost anything or anyone that is set apart for the Lord's purposes.

In the New Testament, the word for *holy* has an even deeper meaning than *qadash,* and understanding it will add depth to our study. The word *hagios* is the Greek word for holy in the New Testament. Absorb the meaning of this word with me. *Hagios* "signifies separated, and hence, in Scripture, separated from sin and therefore consecrated to God, sacred. It expresses something more and higher than sacred, outwardly associated with God; something more than worthy, honorable; something more than pure, free from defilement. *Hagios* is more comprehensive. It is characteristically godlikeness."[27]

By the time the New Testament was written, so much of what had been considered to be holy to the people of antiquity had been defiled in hideous ways. This was true especially in the temple, the religious center of the day. The priests, who had been consecrated by God, had morphed into the Pharisees who looked good on the outside, but were filthy on the inside. The temple itself had become a place of business rather than worship. In essence, the holy had become common or ordinary.

Therefore, it is fitting that the Greek word for holy is more comprehensive and deeper in meaning than the original Hebrew word. If something was considered to be holy, it was sacred—but more than sacred. It was honorable and free from defilement. There would be no question about the association with God for a person or object that was considered to be *hagios,* or holy.

- Turn to the following scripture in the New Testament and note the things that should be considered to be *hagios,* or holy. (HINT: there are two holy things detailed in this verse.)

  1 Peter 1:15–16

It is easy for most of us to understand that God is holy. What baffles many Christians is that they, too, are called to be *hagios*. This word is found in some very interesting places in the New Testament. In the following verses, you will need to keep a keen eye out to find the word that means *hagios*.

- Read Romans 1:7 and Romans 8:27 below. Circle the word(s) from these verses that you believe is used for *hagios*.

- Romans 1:7: "To all in Rome who are loved by God and called to be saints."

- Romans 8:27: "And he who searches our hearts knows the mind of the Spirit, because the Spirit intercedes for the saints in accordance with God's will."

Did you find it? It is the word *saints*. Saints—you and me; those who belong to Jesus because we have allowed His blood to cover our sins are considered holy. We are the holy, the *hagios*, the saints of God.

Let me try that label on for size. Saint Leah? Hmm, it just doesn't seem to fit well. When I think of saints, I think of people like Billy Graham or Mother Teresa—but certainly not Leah Adams. Not with a past like mine. What about you? Go ahead; try on the label of "saint." Saint _____. How does it feel? Doesn't feel quite right to you either, huh?

I believe this is one of those times when we must ignore our feelings. The Word of God calls you and me saints, and we must believe that God knows what He is talking about.

This whole saint thing reminds me of my friend, Cindy, and her experience with a piece of clothing called Spanx. For the Spanx-uninitiated among us, allow me to describe this article of torture. Spanx are footless pantyhose that are designed to shape the female body so as to eliminate the extra rolls and lovehandles that appear as we age. Do not be deceived by the harmless-sounding description of Spanx. They are footless pantyhose that are able to compact huge amounts of cellulite because of the incredible compression they exert on the female body.

Enter Cindy and her newly purchased Spanx. Cindy and her family are dressing for church one Sunday morning, and she decides that she will try out her Spanx. She pulls them out of the package and begins the task of wardrobing herself in them. Let me allow her to tell the story in her own words.

> I will never forget that particular Sunday morning. I was getting ready to go to church to worship my Jesus. It was a pretty ordinary Sunday until I decided that I would try out my new Spanx. Spanx are a type of undergarment designed to reshape you. Billed as "Power Panties," the saleswoman at Chico's told me that they would change my life! Wow!
>
> With eager anticipation of the new me with Spanx, I carefully pulled the undies out of their package. Out came something so small that it looked like a pair of footless tights that belonged to a toddler. I looked at the size on the label and checked it against the back of the package. Yes, the size was right. Then I looked for instructions as to how to get into the teeny, tiny power panties. Alas, there were no instructions. I decided that sometimes in order for our lives to be changed, we just have to take

chances. So with much determination, I began the life-changing process of getting into a pair of Spanx.

I put one foot in, then the other. So far, so good. But I have to tell you, this undergarment was nothing like panties—it was more like a girdle with absolutely no elasticity in it. I managed to pull the garment up to my shins, and then it quickly became apparent that I was going to have to work to get them up any further. So I began to hop and tug on the Spanx at the same time. Finally, I was getting somewhere. I hopped and pulled and hopped and pulled and was making great progress. Just as I had almost gotten the Spanx to where they were supposed to be, the unthinkable happened. My feet got tangled up and down I went; sprawled out on the floor, a picture of perfect grace. Oh, the indignity. By that time, I had worked up a sweat with all the hopping and pulling, so I just laid there for a moment, trying to collect myself. I didn't know whether to laugh or cry. Suddenly I understood how those little sausages felt when they were squeezed into their casings.

While I was trying to compose myself in the floor, my husband walked in, looked at me lying in the floor and said, "We are going to be late for church." Without another word, he turned around and went out to the car to wait for me. Not, "Are you okay?" Not, "Sweetie, why are you lying in the floor?" Not even, "Baby, do you need some help?" But, "We are going to be late for church." Like I didn't already know that!" And to make matters worse, I was having a difficult time breathing due to the constriction of the Spanx.[28]

Just like Cindy's Spanx, our holiness does not always feel like it fits us very well. It feels mis-sized, very constricting, and we may even fall trying to wear it. We feel certain that it was not really meant for us, because we feel far from holy and nowhere near a saint. Yet the packaging that comes with our holiness—the very Word of God—says that it is our size. Our job is to stretch and pull and tug and jump until we are clothed in that holiness. Sometimes it will fit better than at other times. Sometimes we may have to lie down in the floor and struggle with our very flesh in order to attire ourselves in our holiness. Very often, we will look up at our heavenly Father and say, "I just can't make it fit." That is when He will look at us with love in His eyes and say, "No, you can't, but I can help you with it." Little by little, as we allow the Holy Spirit to work in and through us, we begin to recognize that holiness does, indeed, fit us. Oh, it will not feel like the perfect fit until we step out of this tent of flesh and into the presence of Christ, but Jesus sees us now as we will one day be—a saint arrayed in holy garments.

What do you and I know of holy? We know that we are meant to be holy, just as God is holy, and that He stands ready to help us clothe ourselves in this holiness. This week, we will place our lives under the microscope of holiness in an attempt to discover areas that need some refining. This week of study will not be easy, but once we are on the other side of it, we will look back at the work we have done and call it good. Not easy, not always fun, but definitely good. See you tomorrow, my fellow saint.

MEDITATION MOMENT: This week of study is crucial to our goal of living a life that builds a godly legacy for the generations that come behind. I encourage you to spend some time now asking the Lord to prepare your heart for what He has to reveal to you this week. Allow me to get you started …

"Heavenly Father, I want to leave a godly legacy for those who come behind me. You call me holy because I am covered by the blood of Jesus. I desire to walk before You in holiness. Please open my eyes to see the areas of my life that need the Holy Spirit to do some house cleaning. Help me to not hold back any area from the scrutiny of the Spirit. I desire to be clean and holy before You."

Continue your talk with the Lord about any specific areas of your life that you know need to be addressed.

Day 2—Goats and Treaties

My husband and I live in the mountains of North Georgia in a small town called Blairsville. The closest major city to Blairsville is Atlanta, which is a two-hour drive. I go to Atlanta at least once a month, and the route I take winds across a mountain and through a series of small towns. Rural America is what I see as I make my way to the big city. One day, as I was traveling to Atlanta, I passed by a house where I saw a most interesting and comical sight. Allow me to set the scene for you.

The house that I passed is one that always has a very interesting assortment of equipment, vehicles, and animals surrounding it. It sits on the side of the road; however, a small ravine is situated between the house and the road. On this particular day, I was driving reasonably slowly, which is quite unusual for me. However, I was behind another car and could not pass at the point where I encountered the house.

As I passed the house, I glanced toward it and saw the usual assortment of dump trucks, campers, and other equipment parked around it. I also saw a dog chained to a tree in the yard. As I looked at the house, I saw what appeared to be a goat on the front porch. I did a double take. Yes, that is exactly what it was. There was a goat—full-grown, with horns, lying on the front porch—resting on the front porch as if it were the family pet. Remember, the dog is chained in the yard, while the goat is relaxing on the front porch.

I laughed out loud at the absurdity of the picture. Goats do not belong on the front porch of a house. The dog belongs on the front porch, but not the goat. As I laughed at the picture before me, the Holy Spirit spoke to me and said, "That is what happens when you are not vigilant about maintaining your holiness, Leah. You end up with things on the front porch of your heart and life that do not belong there."

In Exodus 34, we find the children of Israel being warned by God about allowing goats on their front porches. Well, actually, God did not talk about goats and porches, but I think you will understand my analogy when we dig into this passage.

Join me as we visit with the children of Israel at Mt Sinai. The answers to the following questions will give you the background that you need to understand our focal passage today.

- Where are the Israelites camped according to Exodus 19:1–2?

- After setting up camp, where did Moses go (Exodus 19:3)?

- What major event occurred in Exodus 20:1–17 and Exodus 31:18?

- While Moses was up on the mountain, what was going on back at the base of the mountain (Exodus 32:1–4)?

Exodus 32:1–2 is a very telling passage of Scripture. The Israelites had grown impatient waiting for Moses to return from his meeting with the Lord, and they began demanding that Aaron, Moses' very own brother, make them a god to follow. Pay attention here, because the words are important.

- Fill in the blanks from Exodus 32:1–2: "When the people saw that Moses was so long in coming down from the mountain, they gathered around Aaron and said, "Come, make us _____ who will _____ _____ us. As for this fellow Moses who _____ us up out of Egypt, we don't know what has happened to him."

Instead of worshipping God on their journey from Egypt, the Israelites had shifted their focus and their worship onto Moses. When Moses disappeared up the mountain, the people begged for another god to lead them.

As you read on in Exodus 32, you find that Aaron gives into the request of the people to make them a god. He instructs them to bring their gold earrings to him, and he fashions a golden calf as an idol for them to worship.

It is at this point that a reasonable thought might be, "Aaron, dude, *what are you thinking?*" Why in the world would Aaron do such a thing? The Bible does not give us an answer to that question. What we do know is that Aaron knew pretty quickly that he had really messed up, because in verse 5, we see him building an altar in front of the calf and declaring that there would be a festival to the Lord the next day. Aaron tried to cover his sin and turn something profane into something holy. That simply cannot be done on a human level. Holiness demands 100% allegiance to God. Nothing less will do.

Let's return to building background. God gives Moses the Ten Commandments and the Law and says, "You'd better get back down there, but you are *not* going to like what you find."

- Several things happened in Exodus 32:19–20. List them here.

After Moses dealt with Aaron and the people, God called him back up on Mt. Sinai to get a second set of tablets with the Commandments on them. Before Moses went back up on the mountain, he had a holy encounter with God in which God told Moses in no uncertain terms that He had just about had it with the Israelites. God promised in Exodus 33 to send the Israelites and his angel on to the Promised Land, but that His presence would not—could not—go with them because of their rebellion, sin, and lack of holiness. Moses begged God to relent and go with the children of Israel into the Promised Land. God had mercy on Moses and the Israelites and agreed to go.

- Read Exodus 34:8–12. What did God clearly instruct Moses and the Israelite *not* to do in verse 12?

- What does verse 12 tell us would happen if they disobeyed this command of God?

God told the Israelites that they were never to make a treaty with the inhabitants of the land. If they disobeyed Him and entered into a treaty, then the people with which they made the agreement would become a snare to them and cause them to sin.

The Hebrew word used for treaty is *beriyt,* and it means "covenant, a marriage covenant between husband and wife."[29] God was telling the people of Israel that making a covenant with the people of the land was a very serious matter. That treaty or covenant would bind them to those people just as a marriage ceremony or covenant binds a husband and wife together.

Any treaty they made with the people in the land would become a snare or a noose around their neck. God promised that ultimately that noose would tighten and they would be destroyed because of the treaty. God gave His stiff-necked and rebellious people a clear warning—yet as we read throughout the Old Testament, we find that they did the very thing against which He had warned them.

My friends, we in this generation have made treaties with the inhabitants of this land. God calls us to holy living, yet all too often, we look no different than the world. The call to holiness requires that we be different than those around us. Holy living says that we dress modestly, speak reverently, and live cleanly before God. All too often, Christians blend in, fit in, and compromise in with those who live in this world, and this becomes a snare to us.

You and I must never forget that God hates sin. It all comes down to obedience. Consider this quote from *The Pursuit of Holiness* by Jerry Bridges: "We become so accustomed to our sins we sometimes lapse into a peaceful co-existence with them, but God never ceases to hate them."[30]

As Christians, we must be stronger in our faith, bolder in our witness, uncompromising in our character, and purer in our holiness if we desire to leave a godly legacy for the generations that come behind us. Is there a goat resting on the front porch of your heart that desperately needs to be put out in the pasture of the world where he belongs? Holiness is *your* choice.

MEDITATION MOMENT: Choose one of the following verses pertaining to holiness and commit it to memory this week: Leviticus 11:44a; Leviticus 11:45; 1 Peter 1:15–16

Day 3 – Dress for Success

Hands down, it qualifies as the worst vacation I have ever taken. Greg and I had only been married a short while, and we decided to go to San Francisco for a long weekend. I had lived for a few months in the Bay area earlier in my single life and wanted to show him the beauty of the California coast. We left home, eager to enjoy some time away seeing San Francisco. *That* is where the trouble began.

I had purchased what I considered to be a very cute, short denim wrap dress for the trip. I decided to wear it to travel to San Francisco. I put it on, along with a pair of sandals, and out the door we went. I noticed that Greg was very quiet on our drive to the Atlanta airport, but my excitement about our vacation caused me to dismiss his quietness completely. When we arrived at the airport, we checked our baggage and began the very long walk to the gate where we would board our plane. I noticed that Greg walked several paces behind me the entire time, but again, I did not give it much thought.

We arrived in San Francisco, collected our bags, got the rental car, and made our way to our hotel. By this time, it was obvious that something was not right with Greg. We got into our hotel room, and I said to him, "You have been very quiet, and you walked behind me, rather than with me, most of the day. Is something wrong?

Greg proceeded to inform me that my very cute dress was way too short and revealed things that should not be revealed. He suggested that I looked like one of Rahab's co-workers, if you know what I mean!

I was offended and incredibly angry with him. I had not purposely set out to look like a prostitute, and I told him so in no uncertain terms. He reasoned that obviously I had, since I had chosen to wear the dress that I was wearing. We argued for a long while with no resolution. I was not backing down, and neither was he. I said that maybe I should just get on a plane and go home. He said that maybe he should too, because he had no intention of being embarrassed by the way I dressed for the entire vacation. Neither of us did, but it was mighty quiet in our hotel room for most of the trip.

At the time I did not realize how on target he was, nor would I have admitted it. I did not view my dress as inappropriate or more revealing than outfits worn by any other twenty-somethings living in the mid-nineties. From my front view in the full-length mirror, the dress hit me at mid-thigh. Because the dress was a wrap style, the view from the back was obviously very different—and that was the crux of the problem.

- Read 1 Corinthians 10:23. Now write out what you understand the verse to mean.

Paul tells us that just because the world says that it is acceptable to do something, that does not necessarily mean that doing that thing is acceptable behavior for a Christian. Ouch! "But, but"—no buts.

Ponder what Titus says about the behavior of Christian women. In Titus 2:3–5, God instructs older women to teach the younger women how to live reverent lives. Listen to this passage from The *Message:* "Guide older women into lives of reverence so they end up as neither gossips nor drunks, but models of goodness. By looking at them, the younger women will know how to love their husbands and children, be virtuous and pure, keep a good house, be good wives. We don't want anyone looking down on God's Message because of their behavior."[31]

At this point, you may say to me, "Leah, those verses do not say one thing about how a woman should dress." You would be right—partially. Keep these verses in mind for a few minutes, because we will come back to them. First I want to share some thoughts with you—my own, as well as the thoughts of other men and women.

When Greg and I argued about the intent of my dress on that day in San Francisco, we were both right. Truly, I had no intention of looking like a prostitute. I simply had no idea how the way I dressed was perceived.

In her eye-opening book, *For Women Only: What You Need to Know About the Inner Lives of Men*, Shaunti Feldhahn discusses the results of a survey that she commissioned. The survey was a blind, random, well-planned and well-executed study of 400 anonymous men from all across the United States. These men ranged in age from 21 to 75. They answered twenty-four questions about their lives and what they think, feel, and need. She followed this initial survey up with an informal survey directed toward 400 additional men. Later, Feldhahn performed another blind, random survey to validate what she had found in the two initial surveys.

Most of us doing this Bible study have probably heard that men are far more visual than women. I'm not sure most women understand what that means. Let me allow Shaunti to tell you in her own words from her book: "Here's the insight that I stumbled on by accident, which has radically reshaped my understanding of men: Even happily married men are instinctively pulled to visually 'consume' attractive women, and these images can be just as alluring whether they are live or recollected."[32]

One of the questions posed to these men by Feldhahn was, "Imagine you are sitting alone in a train station and a woman with a great body walks in and stands in a nearby line. What is your reaction to the woman?" The men were given four choices of answers:

1. I openly stare at her, and drool forms on my lower lip;

2. I'm drawn to look at her, and I sneak a peek or glance at her from the corner of my eye;

3. It is impossible not to be aware that she is there, but I try to stop myself from looking; and

4. Nothing happens; it doesn't affect me.[33]

Ninety-eight percent of the men said that responses 2 or 3 were accurate for them! (76% answered number 2, while 18% answered number 3). Only 2% said that they would not be affected by this woman with a great body.

Shaunti says, "Interestingly, the results were essentially the same for men who described themselves as happily married believers."[34] She describes that, because of how their brains are wired, even the most godly men are tempted to want to look - even if they do the right thing and don't.

She goes on to say that men have a mental Rolodex of sensual images stored in their minds. For those among us who don't know what a Rolodex is, consider it to be a filing cabinet for the sake of this discussion.

Listen—really listen—to what Shaunti says next. This is what made me realize that the way I was dressing—regardless of whether the rest of the world was dressing this way or not—was wrong.

> We've all heard that the male half of the population thinks about sex a lot. What I didn't realize was that they aren't exactly *thinking* about sex *(as in, I wonder if my wife will be in the mood tonight)*. Rather, they're *picturing* it, or picturing a sexual image. And those pictures aren't, unfortunately, always of their wives. They are often images that have been involuntarily burned in their brains just by living in today's culture—images that can arise without warning.
>
> You might be wondering, *What* kinds *of images?* Apparently just about anything: the memory of an intimate time with you (good) or the memory of a *Playboy* magazine (bad). It could be a recollection of a shapely woman who walked through the parking lot two minutes ago or an online porn site he saw two years ago. These images often arise in his brain without warning, *even if the guy doesn't want them there.* Or specific images can be recalled on purpose. As several men put it, "I have an unending supply of images in my head, stretching back to my teens."[35]

Girls, do you see where I am going here? My husband knew that day in San Francisco exactly what Shaunti discovered. Although I had not intended to be a sexual image in some man's mind, I might very well have ended up being one simply because of the way I was dressed. I fear that too many of us have unwittingly ended up in the mental Rolodex of men because of the choices we make in clothing.

I'm not suggesting that we go back to the era of long dresses and chin-high collars. What I am suggesting is that we be very conscious of the length of our skirts and shorts, the tightness of our pants and blouses, and the amount of cleavage that shows. We can dress in an attractive, fashionable way without looking like a hooker, ladies. We can, and we must—not only for our sakes, but for the sakes of the men around us. We do not want to cause a man to fall into temptation by the way we are dressed. Shaunti found that even if a man does the right thing and wrenches his eyes and thoughts away, it is a daily struggle in this culture—a struggle a man was never supposed to have to face. After all, the only intimate image he was ever supposed to have burned into his brain was that of his wife!

When we choose to dress in clothes that are too short, too tight, or too revealing, we cheapen the temple in which God resides. The temple that Solomon built for the Lord in the Old Testament became one of the Seven Wonders of the Ancient Word. It was beautiful and grand and reverent. When we offer the Holy Spirit a cheapened, sexualized temple in which to live, we offer less than our best to the One who died to save us.

Finally, look back at the verses from Titus 2 that we read earlier in today's study. Consider that final sentence: "We don't want anyone looking down on God's Message because of their behavior." Do you want to cause others to look down on God's Message because of the way that you dress? Or do you desire to be a beautiful, godly representative of the Lord Jesus Christ in a world that desperately needs to see Him? It's your choice. Dress for success in the Kingdom of God.

MEDITATION MOMENT: Ask the Lord to show you if you need to make changes in the way that you dress so that you are honoring Him. If you have daughters or granddaughters, ask the Lord to help you talk with them about this issue of modesty. This is such an important part of the legacy that you are leaving for future generations.

Day 4—Disobedience and Regrets

What is your biggest regret in life? What is the one thing that, if you had a do-over, you would do differently?

This is the question that I posed in late 2009 to those who read my blog. The answers that I received are quite telling as we think about this issue of holiness and our legacy. A significant portion of the answers pertained to sexual sin committed by the respondent, and that is what I would like for us to ponder today.

Allow me to share a few of the anonymous responses with you.

"The biggest regret in my life is the sexual sin that I lived in for so many years. I used sex as a way to get what I perceived would be love, but it never was. I regret misusing the temple of the Holy Spirit in such horrendous ways. Major regret!"

"My biggest regret has to be sexual sin. I know I am forgiven and redeemed, and I am so thankful for that. But I so wish I didn't have memories of other guys—wish my husband really was my 'one and only.'"

"My biggest regret is that for so many years I lived as if I was not a Christian. I squandered my inheritance, so to speak, by ungodly living, sexual sin, you name it. It would have been a wonderful thing to present myself to my husband on our wedding day undefiled."

"My biggest regret has been sexual sin. I was twenty-one years old, in college, and still a virgin. I believed the lie that my virginity made me weird, and I convinced myself that losing my virginity was no big deal. I lost my virginity that same year to a man I thought I loved. How *stupid!* How I wish I had remained pure for my husband."[36]

Regret over sexual sin. Perhaps you can identify with the words of these women. I know I certainly can. All too often, we—like Eve in the Garden of Eden—believe Satan's lie that God's commands bind us and keep us from having fun and living life to the fullest. What a monumental lie that is! God's commands are for our good. If you don't believe it, go back and look carefully at the answers those precious ladies gave to my question. If those ladies had followed God's commands concerning sexual purity, there would be no regret over misusing the temple of the Holy Spirit. Nor would there be regret over coming to their husband on their wedding night as a used vessel.

I believe this issue of sexual purity is one that hinders the holiness of many Christians. Let's peer into God's Word and see what it has to tell us on this issue.

The writer of Holy Scripture is only two chapters in when He begins to talk about this issue of sexual purity. Consider what He says in Genesis 2:24, and fill in the blanks.

- For this reason a man will leave his father and mother and be united to his _____, and they will become _____flesh.

Notice in this verse that it is only after being united in marriage that the man and the woman become one flesh. This verse evidences a natural progression for sexual intimacy. Marriage comes first; sexual intimacy follows.

In this verse, we see that sexual intimacy causes the man and the woman to become *one* flesh. This joining together of a man and a woman sexually causes a bond to be built between them. Picture two glasses, one containing water and one containing milk. If we pour both glasses of liquid into a pitcher, they become one liquid, and it is impossible to separate the water from the milk. So it is with sexual intimacy where the two individuals become one flesh, each now joined to the other, whether in marriage or out.

If you are sexually active with anyone other than your marriage partner, then you have a bond with that person, and you bring a bit of them into the marriage with you. This is true whether we are dealing with pre-marital sex or extra-marital sex—what the Bible rightly terms adultery. Remember the lady who wished she didn't have the memories of the other men with whom she had been intimate? She brought those men with her into her marriage.

God is very clear that our bodies belong to our husband in 1 Corinthians 7:4. Yet if we have given part of them away to other sexual partners, we live in our marriage as less than a whole person. This defrauds our husband of what is rightfully his. We have not only cheated our mate, but ourselves as well, for we have settled for far less than God desired for us in our marriage.

Engaging in sexual intimacy outside of marriage is not God's plan, and He will never bless it. Never. I have heard women attempt to justify affairs and pre-marital sex by saying that they believe God wants them to be happy, and this is the way to be happy. Engaging in sexual intimacy outside of a marriage relationship is absolute disobedience to the commands of God, and there will be consequences for those actions. Nowhere is God more clear about this than in 1 Thessalonians 4:3–5. Read 1 Thessalonians 4:3–4 and answer the following question:

- What three things are detailed as being God's will?

God's will is that we control our body so that we will live a holy life according to verse 7. A holy life, rather than an impure and disobedient life, is what God desires for us.

- When we choose not to live in God's will, who does verse 8 say that we are really hurting and rejecting?

At this point, many of you might be thinking, "Leah, don't be so old-fashioned. If I want to be sexually intimate, it is my business—not yours." And I would say, "You are right. It is your business." However, I want to be sure that you have thought carefully about the consequences of your actions. Most of us have that "it'll never happen to me" mentality about this issue of sexual impropriety. But what if it does happen to you?

What if:

- you get caught?

- you get pregnant?

- you catch a sexually transmitted disease like herpes, genital warts, or AIDS?

- you are used and thrown away like a dirty rag?

- your reputation and character are ruined by your actions?

Please do not be so naïve as to think, "It won't happen to me," because it can—and it most likely will.

- Fill in the blanks from Galatians 6:7: "Do not be _____: God cannot be _____. A man _____what he _____."

Listen to this verse from *The Message:* "Don't be misled: No one makes a fool of God. What a person plants, he will harvest."[37] Think about it this way: if I desire a harvest of squash, I must plant squash seeds. It does me no good to plant geranium seeds in hope of getting squash. It just will not happen. Like begets like.

If I desire a loving, intimate relationship with my husband, I cannot go out and have an affair with another man and expect my relationship with my husband to blossom and bloom. I will reap what I have sown, and what I reap will be discord, unhappiness, and deceit.

Not only will I reap what I sow, but I will reap more than I sow and later than I sow. The perceived pleasure of an improper sexual relationship only lasts for a short while, but the consequences of those actions are multiplied and lasting.

God will *not* allow you to live in sin without consequences. Sex outside of marriage is *sin*—no other way to say it. It is blatant rebellion against God, and He will not allow it to continue without consequences. I cannot tell you what the consequences will be, but I can assure you that you will wish you had not gone down the path of rebellion against Him.

So what is the good news? There is good news if you are willing to resist sexual temptation or turn away from blatant sexual sin.

- Turn to Isaiah 55:6–7. List the four action verbs in these verses.

God says we are to seek Him and call out to Him in repentance. He then desires for us to forsake the sin so that we can walk before Him in holiness.

- Verse 7 promises two things to those who seek, call, and forsake. What are they?

My friend, God stands ready to not only forgive the sin of sexual impurity, but He will do exactly what King David asked Him to do for himself after he confessed his sin of adultery.

- Turn to Psalm 51. Write verses 10–12 in the margin. The spoken word has incredible power. Please repeat these verses out loud now.

Friends, I hope that today's lesson has been one that you cannot identify with at all. My desire is that you have always remained faithful to God's design for sexual purity and that you are reaping the harvest of blessings for your obedience.

However, if you have not always followed God's plan for sexual purity, I pray that you have found God faithful to call you back to Himself and offer forgiveness and restoration for your sin. If you are engaging in an improper sexual relationship, I beg you, please stop! Whatever pleasure you find in it will never outweigh the dreadful consequences. You cannot leave a godly legacy for those who come behind you if you are choosing disobedience to God in this area of your life. Please count the cost of your actions.

MEDITATION MOMENT: Each of us knows at least one young woman between the ages of thirteen and twenty-five. Choose a young woman in this age group. Write her initials here. _____ Commit to pray for her and her sexual purity. Your prayers for this young woman are an important part of the legacy that you will leave behind.

Day 5—Shun the Appearance of Evil

Recently I spoke at a ladies conference where my message was *this* message: the legacy that we are leaving for the generations that come behind us. In that message, I talked about the fact that we need to be very conscious regarding the appearance of evil. I gave the example of allowing ourselves to be alone in a room with a man who is not our husband. Even though the situation may be innocent enough, there is risk involved, and Satan loves to capitalize on just those types of situations.

During the post-event luncheon, one of the beautiful ladies at my table looked at me and said, "Leah, may I ask you a question?"

I said, "Of course."

"I had never considered the issue of being alone in a room with a man who is not my husband," she mused. "I'm not sure how I would do that."

"Why?" I asked.

She explained that she is a musician, and very often she is in the recording studio working on music with her producer who is a man and there are no other people in the room.

"Are there other people in the building?" I inquired.

"Yes, there are," she replied.

"One way to make this work is to leave the door to the room open, if there are no windows in the door," I suggested. "However, if there are no windows in the door and you cannot leave the door open, then you must make a choice. Either bring someone into the room as a third party, or find a different way to work with this man."

I'm not sure she was excited about what I said. Oddly enough, this woman is not an exception to the rule. I've had this same conversation with other women who had never considered the dangers of being alone in a room with a man who is not their husband. Neither had I until several years ago.

Before I go further, let me clarify that the phrase "shun the very appearance of evil" does not appear anywhere in the Bible. Today's lesson is about seeking discernment as we work to elevate our holiness factor in life. We will see that there are many situations in life that call for discernment and wisdom. My goal is to encourage you to give some thought to those situations *before* you find yourself in them.

Let's ponder some other circumstances where we should heed the advice to shun the appearance of evil. I'll list a few for your consideration; then I'll ask you to come up with some of your own.

- You are solely responsible for the finances of the company where you work. You have little accountability in matters such as check-writing or funds disbursement.

- You are a teacher who often is alone in the room with a student.

- You frequently visit mixed-sex chat rooms online.

- You read steamy romance novels or allow your daughter to read them.

- You are a physician or mental health practitioner who serves patients in confidential situations.

Okay, now it's your turn. Write a few examples of situations where the advice to shun the appearance of evil should be heeded.

The prophet Isaiah warned about those who refuse to see evil or the potential for evil for what it is. Even 2,700 years ago, the tendency to think, "Nothing is going to happen, because I can handle this situation" was alive and well.

- Turn to Isaiah 5:20–21 and fill in the blanks: "_____ to those who call _____good and good _____, who put _____ for light and light for _____, who put _____ for sweet and sweet for _____. _____to those who are _____in their own eyes and _____in their own sight."

When we refuse to count the cost or even the potential cost of our actions; when we try to call what is evil good; when we pridefully and falsely think we will never fall—God says "woe" to us.

King David knew very well the consequences of failing to count the cost. He failed miserably when it came to shunning the very appearance of evil, and there was a devastating impact to his family for generations.

Turn to 2 Samuel 11 and read all twenty-seven verses. Please read this passage carefully, looking for places where King David should have employed our focal phrase, "Shun the appearance of evil." I'll wait here for you to return.

Welcome back! I want us to glance at two places in this story where David could have chosen to walk away from a situation that later led to his downward spiral into sin and tragedy.

- In 2 Samuel 11:1, what was the traditional ritual that occurred in the springtime?

- Also in this verse, who went to war that year?

- Where was David?

David, the king of Israel, should have been leading the armies of Israel out to war. Yet he abandoned his position and decided to stay home. This is the equivalent of Bill Gates deciding that he is going to take a break from running Microsoft at a very crucial time in the life of the company, letting his second-in-command take charge. While the second-in-commands in Gates's organization and in David's kingdom may be very capable men, they are not the person who has the vision and who is supposed to be in charge.

Plain and simple, David shirked his responsibility as king of Israel. God had placed him as king of Israel and entrusted the running of the kingdom to him. Yet in a crucial hour, David fails to be faithful to fulfill the duty placed on him by the Lord. Although this may seem like a small thing to you and me, it is the beginning of the end for David's holiness at this season of his life, as we see in the remainder of the chapter.

The second place that we discover where David could have taken care to shun the appearance of evil is in verse 2 of this same chapter.

- Complete the sentence from verse 2: "One evening David got up from his bed and walked around on the roof of the palace. From the roof he _____ a woman bathing."

This is one of those parts of Scripture that causes me to want to ask a lot of questions. Questions like, "What was David doing up on the roof of the palace?" and "Why was Bathsheba taking a bath on the roof of her house?" I just want to know the answers to these questions, for heaven's sake.

The Bible says that from the palace roof he saw a woman bathing. We will find that the Hebrew meaning of the word "saw" adds an entirely new dimension to the story. It helps us understand why this is a place where David should have shunned the very appearance of evil.

The Hebrew word for "saw" is *ra'ah,* and it means "to see, look at, inspect, perceive, consider."[38] According to the Hebrew, David did not just casually glance at this woman bathing on her roof. He stopped and inspected. He gazed and allowed his gaze to linger. When David should have been inspecting troops in battle, his eyes were scrutinizing a bathing beauty who belonged to someone else. In the moment when David should have been high-tailing it back into the palace in order to head out to battle, he was instead sending a servant to inquire about this woman.

In three verses, we see three situations where David failed to shun the appearance of evil and pursue holiness. At each of these places, David could have made a decision to do something different. He could have led the Israelite army to battle. He could have turned his eyes away when he saw the woman bathing. He could have refrained from sending someone to find out about this woman. He could have—but he didn't. Ultimately, David's failure to shun the appearance of evil led him to commit adultery, deception, and murder.

Shunning the appearance of evil is really a matter of being obedient to what God calls us to do and be. The Holy Spirit will never lead us into a situation that will cause us to sin. It is our choice whether we will follow the leading of the Spirit or choose our own way.

In his marvelously insightful book, *The Pursuit of Holiness,* Jerry Bridges says the following about this issue of obedience and disobedience as it pertains to holiness: "It is time for us Christians to face up to our responsibility for holiness. Too often we say we are 'defeated' by this sin or that sin. No, we are not defeated; we are simply disobedient! It might be well if we stopped using the terms 'victory' and 'defeat' to describe our progress in holiness. Rather we should use the terms 'obedience' and 'disobedience' … when I say I am defeated by some sin, I am unconsciously slipping out from under my responsibility. I am saying something outside of me has defeated me. But when I say I am disobedient, that places the responsibility for my sin squarely on me."[39]

Obedience or disobedience. Holiness or unholiness. The choice is ours, and that choice will greatly impact the legacy that we leave for the generations that come behind us. Let's choose to shun the very appearance of evil in our lives.

MEDITATION MOMENT: Has the Holy Spirit spoken to you today about anything in your life toward which you need to apply today's lesson on the value of shunning the appearance of evil? If so, please take time right now to ask the Lord to help you walk in obedience to Him and to turn away from anything that could lead you into sin.

Week 6 –Trash Pile to Treasure Chest—Legacies to Consider

Well, my friend, here we are. The final week of our time together—and what a journey it has been! We have pondered the meaning of the word *legacy* and examined the lives of Bible characters as they built their own legacies. Our hearts were stirred as we considered the faith walks of the great people in the Bible, as well as our own. We allowed the Holy Spirit to prick our consciences through an evaluation of our character where each of us likely saw areas that could use some cleaning up. Last week, our holiness was placed under God's microscope to ensure that our lives mirror the life of Christ Jesus. Whew! Girlfriend, we have done some work—and frankly, I am sad that we are at the end.

I have asked the Father to have a major impact on your life as we have taken this journey. Although I know that the study of God's Word *never* fails to have an impact, I really want for you to close the book on this study knowing that you are building a godly legacy. My desire is that you have recognized at least one area of your life where improvements could be made. This is my hope—because really, none of us have got this legacy-building thing down as long as we are breathing the pollen-filled air of earth.

My goal for our time together this week is to provide you with real-life examples of women who are walking this legacy-building thing out each and every day of their lives. As we hear their stories, we will find a transparency about them with regard to their successes *and* their failures that I believe will encourage us to press on in our own pursuit of godly legacies.

Yes, I said failures. I've asked them to be candidly honest about where they succeeded and where they failed in this legacy-building endeavor. I did this because it is important for us to understand that there *will* be times when we fail miserably at living a life that leaves a godly legacy. Simply put, on occasion, most of us will make a mess of our lives that would make a two-year-old proud. The good news is that God does not give up on us. If we allow it, He picks us up, dusts us off, and says, "Get back in the game, girl. You've got a legacy to build."

As a manager in the medical world, one of my hard-and-fast rules was that I would never ask someone to do something that I was unwilling to do. So on Day 1, I will offer you my story of the successes and failures of my own legacy-building endeavor. Hang on! It gets ugly before it gets pretty.

Week 6 Goals:

- Visit with three women as they share their legacy-building stories

- Perform a legacy checkup on your own heart

Day 1—I Did It My Way

When I was fifteen, I realized that I needed Jesus to come into my heart and be the boss, the king, and the ruler of my life. I asked Him to come into my heart, live forever, and help me to live a life that pleased Him. Wonderful! As we studied in Week 1, that is the perfect beginning for building a godly legacy. With a few notable exceptions, my legacy-building efforts went downhill from there.

At the age of twenty-one, I married my high school sweetheart. I use the word "sweetheart" very loosely. The day I walked down the aisle of my church on my father's arm, I recall thinking, "What am I doing? I don't want to marry him." The problem was that I was physically sick—ravaged by the effects of an ongoing battle with anorexia. Add to that the psychological issues that go along with an obsessive-compulsive disorder, and you have quite a mess. I did not have the physical or emotional stamina to make a different decision. My family liked him, and so I married him.

That began three of the worst years of my life, and the emotional trauma was huge. Psychological abuse is a different animal. The abused has no physical marks to offer as evidence, yet the abuse is very real. Truth be told, I was probably not far from considering suicide, because I knew that barring some miracle, I could not live the rest of my life in that situation. I cried almost every day of those three years, either silently in my heart or aloud to my God.

In the final weeks of my marriage, I engaged in an extra-marital affair that caused me to end the marriage and perhaps save my life. Please know that in *no way* am I seeking to justify the adultery that I committed. It was a sin against God and the man to whom I was married. I had to ask for God's forgiveness, but I found Him faithful to provide forgiveness.

I divorced in 1988 and very nearly rushed into marriage with the man with whom I had the affair. He did not know Jesus as his Lord and Savior. It would have been that whole "unequally yoked" thing that Paul talks about in 2 Corinthians 6:14.

This verse is so important to us as we think about building a legacy that I would like for you to take a moment to look up the verse.

- Write out 2 Corinthians 6:14 here.

- Now circle the words in this verse that describe unbelievers.

Perhaps I am taking a bit of theological license here, but I want to use two of the words out of this verse to make a point. The words are *common* and *fellowship*. In the Greek, the word for *fellowship* is *metoche*, and it means "a sharing, communion, fellowship." I don't know about you, but it is difficult for me to sit down and fellowship over a meal or a cup of coffee with someone with whom I have absolutely nothing in common. Alternatively, I may meet a person who I have never met before but who is a believer in Jesus Christ, and we instantly sense a bond because of the Lord.

This is an oversimplified way to describe what happens when a believer in Christ marries or in any way aligns themselves with unbelievers. There simply is nothing in common. It is like comparing apples and oranges; like trying to fit a square peg in a round hole; like mixing water and oil. None of these are a good fit—they don't mix well. Oh, they may co-exist and even be amicable, but ultimately there will be friction or problems because the two were never meant to become one.

Back to my post-divorce affair. I truly believe God prevented that relationship from moving forward. I was so desperately needy at that time that I nearly smothered everyone in my path who showed me the least bit of attention. You see, I was looking for a man to fill my needs when I should have been looking to Jesus alone for that filling. So many of us make that mistake, girls. We get it into our color-treated heads that a created man can fill our every need and make us deliriously happy forever. Without a doubt, men are wonderful blessings from God; but no man was ever meant to meet every need that a woman has. Only Jesus is qualified and capable of doing that.

In the months after my divorce, I began to learn—for the first time in my life—exactly who I was. I had never lived alone and had never supported myself. Thankfully, my parents had supplied me with a fantastic education so that I could support myself financially. I had a good job, good friends, and a good church to support me. The wise thing to do would have been to walk with God and find my self-worth in Him. Unfortunately, that is not what I did. I am slow learner!

For the next six years, I engaged in horrendously sinful behavior. Although I remained engaged in church, it was mostly to assuage guilt for my behavior throughout the week. The singles scene in Atlanta offered a great deal of excitement and thrill, and I partook of it generously. Sexual sin, liberal use of alcohol, inappropriate dress, the use of profanity, and so much more quenched any evidence of the Lord in my life. The consequences of that lifestyle were huge, both physically and emotionally. Spiritually, I hungered for God and the joy that came from walking with Him. Yet I was too enamored with living life my own way. Did I mention there was rampant sexual sin in my life in those days? The scars left by that season are visible to me yet today, fifteen years into a wonderful marriage to an awesome Christian man.

I am a living, breathing testimony to Galatians 6:7, which I paraphrase here: "Do not be deceived, God will not be mocked. As a girl sows, so shall she reap." And boy, did I reap the consequences of the lifestyle that I chose! I suppose I thought that I would be *the one* who would not have to reap the consequences of disobedience. How wrong I was!

But … what a wonderful word! But. However. In spite of.

But one day I got so weary and sick of the way I was living that I decided something had to change. The CliffsNotes version of the story is that God sent a wonderful man to me who would become my husband. I recognized that God's hand was all over this relationship, and slowly—very slowly—I began the climb out of the pit that I had dug for myself. The first years of our marriage were difficult at best, because I had a lot of healing and repairing that needed to take place in my life in order for me to be whole. Finally I began moving in the right direction.

In 2001, the Holy Spirit placed in my heart a hunger and a rabid desire for the Word of God unlike anything I had ever experienced. It was a desire as strong as any physical thirst I had ever known. I could not get enough of Jesus and His Word. I prayed and studied the Bible using guided, in-depth studies by incredible authors such as Beth Moore, Jennifer Rothschild, Priscilla Shirer, Max Lucado, and so many more. I found in Christ what I had been seeking from men for so many years. Hear that again—I found *in Christ* what I had been seeking *from men* for so many years: a relationship that was deep and abiding and eternal. I found fulfillment and contentment and joy.

Did my thoughts, actions, and words change overnight? In most cases, no. What I discovered was that as I continued to dig into the Bible and embed God's truth in my heart, my thoughts, actions, and words began to change. I remember thinking one day, "I haven't used a curse word in weeks." What had happened? God had replaced my foul language with His Words. As I began to find my worth and value in Christ, I had no more desire to seek it from sinful sexual relationships with men. Jesus provided inestimable value and worth to a life that had previously felt worthless because of the sin I had lived in for so long.

Allow me to share with you a Bible verse that the Lord used during this time to draw me closer to Him and ingrain His truth in my heart.

- Look up 2 Timothy 2:13, write it out completely, and summarize in your own words what God is saying. Yes, you read that correctly. First write out the entire verse. Then summarize it in your own words.

I needed to know that. Despite my failure to act with character, integrity, and holiness, God will always be faithful to what He had promised. What had He promised? He had promised that because I asked Jesus to be the boss, the king, and the ruler of my heart, He would *never* forsake me. God would never grow so disgusted with my behavior that He would say, "Enough. I've had enough of her and her rebellion. Away with her!"

No, my loving heavenly Father was always waiting—longing—for me to return to Him. And when I did—oh, the joy, the passion, the love that I found.

What do I want my legacy to be when I am gone from this earth? I want others to remember that I loved Jesus with all my heart. I want them to know that no matter how far away they walk from God, He never walks away from us if we are His children through the blood of Jesus. Never! I want my life to be characterized by obedience to God and His Word until the day I breathe my last on this dusty trail of earth.

My life verse is Psalm 3:3. It is a one-verse short story about what God has done in my life. "But you are a shield around me, O Lord; you bestow glory on me and lift up my head." Indeed, God has been a shield around me so often when I walked blindly into trouble. He offers to share His glory with me, which astounds me when I think of my background. Finally, He lifts up my head. Satan would have me walk around in shame and despair over the choices that I have made. Yet the Father places His holy hand beneath my chin, gently raises my head so that my eyes meet His, and says, "You are my daughter; my princess. Enjoy the benefits that your Father provides for you."

God offers the same to you. Will you accept His offer?

MEDITATION MOMENT: What part of my legacy story speaks to your heart? Why?

Day 2—Channy's Story

What a joy it is to introduce you to my friend, Channy. Actually, her real name is Cheryl Ann, but we all know her as Channy (pronounced "Shanny" with a short 'a'). She is a wonderful wife, mother, and friend. Her four beautiful children have been "raised right," as my grandmother would have said. Channy is a nurse whose primary passions are her family and her God.

It is my honor to have her share the story of her legacy-building efforts with us today. I am confident that you will find parts of her story that reach out and touch your heart. Please join me in welcoming my precious friend to our Bible study.

> I was born the fourth of nine children into a low-middle-class family in the Rocky Mountains of Montana. My mother was a devout Protestant, while my father lived most of his life as a hard-working, agnostic, beer-drinking, cursing man. They loved all of their children and reared us the best way they knew how. I came to know Jesus as my Savior at about age eight and was baptized in a creek in the summer as water flowed down from the snowy mountains that ringed the valley. I did not completely understand what it really meant to be saved, but I prayed a lot to Jesus in those early years. There were conflicting value systems that were being lived out in front of me by my parents, and my heart needed to make sense of them.
>
> Unfortunately, my salvation was not followed by the discipleship that teaches the importance of studying God's Word each day. My spiritual training consisted of the things that my mother taught me, as well as the words of the pastor of our tiny church. I think I always believed that if I didn't abide by the rules, I would be back to

square one and on the outs with God. I suppose I believed that I'd lose my salvation if I did not behave.

My mother's portrayal of the Christian life always reminded me of Hollywood's portrayal of the black slaves in early America. The hymns she continuously sang were in a flat monotone, devoid of joy—which reflected her view of earth as a place to be endured as a martyr until Jesus relieved you of your heavy burden. Mom is a Native American half-breed who grew up in a generation of discrimination. She developed a stubborn, pride-filled martyr's attitude to cover the pain and insecurity she felt. Even her rendition of "Jesus Loves Me" sounded like a sad Negro spiritual as she wearily rocked the babies to sleep.

Daddy was always busy and overworked. In order to make ends meet and feed eleven mouths, he volunteered for any overtime that was offered at the lumber mill. His fingernails were never clean of black grease until at least a year after he retired. I think he was unbearably tired and despondent because of his life situation. Alcohol, restoring old cars, and stealing away frequently to sit at a bar with other weary men were his escape from the life that was laid out before him. No one in our family doubted Dad's love for us. What we were never able to find in Dad—until his final years on earth—was a love for Jesus.

I was a bright, naturally academic child, and I excelled in my schoolwork. My three older siblings were not as blessed, and I quickly developed a prideful attitude concerning my talents. Mom knew God didn't like pride—and neither did she.

Daddy was proud of my accomplishments in his own quiet way. He had dropped out of school in the eighth grade to make his way in the world and escape from his harsh childhood, and I believe he found vicarious pleasure in my accomplishments. Because of my pride, I felt rejected by my mother and longed for the love and affirmation of my father. This created a formula for self-destruction. I caught the eye of older boys and quickly was wooed by the pledges of love and forever. I engaged in sex at a young age and was betrayed and wounded. To complicate matters, I was oblivious to the fact that my Bible contained the love letters I wanted desperately to receive. I resorted to a host of meaningless sexual relationships which caused me to build a wall around my heart. I was always hoping that the next man would find he could not live without me. As deceitful, guilty, and clandestine as my depraved life became, I still managed to maintain stubborn pride and superiority about my academic accomplishments and the fact that I had never tried illegal drugs. Alcoholic indulgences obviously were acceptable, because Dad drank, and society seemed to accept it.

I left my hated home town, thinking that if I ran as far as I could, I would leave my hurt, my reputation, my shame behind. On my own in college in Florida, I grabbed onto the first handsome guy I could find and lured him with my sexual prowess, intellect, and my jealous—albeit needy—devotion. I married him at twenty years of age and began climbing the social ladder in order to make a name for myself. My goal was to look good to everyone. I wanted the cars, the house, the clothes, the friends, and the 2.5 children. I continued to excel in school and ultimately graduated from nursing school as a registered nurse. This was all part of maintaining the façade of social acceptability and the image of being successful. My marriage, which produced two children, disintegrated for a host of reasons. It still staggers me that God would entrust me—a prideful, independent (in a bad way), deplorable wretch—with two innocent, beautiful children.

I was thirty years old, divorced, depressed, and desperate. I cried out to God, and He heard me. Soon I married a thirty-three-year-old bachelor who had been waiting anxiously for God to send him a wife. He had his own baggage and guilt, but longed desperately to set his life right. He had been reared in a working-class, Southern Baptist, church-going family. He knew what God wanted for his life, even if he had spent several years looking for it in all the wrong places. He loved me and my young children, and he desired to create a God-centered family.

Over the next few years, God humbled me and broke my stubborn pride. He did this because of His great love for me. When I was broken enough to be of any use to Him, God graciously gave me a chance to be used by Him. The avenue He took me down astounds me.

I was comfortably entrenched in my Bible-based Baptist church, and I finally understood that my salvation wouldn't go down the toilet with my next sin. I was intimately involved in a small, in-depth Bible study and taught a fifth- and sixth-grade mission class at church. My three children were being immersed in Biblical truth and were surrounded by the love and support of our church family. Life was good! God was good! The only dark cloud in my life was (and sometimes still is) my acidic resentment and lack of forgiveness toward my continually irritating and hateful ex-husband.

One Wednesday evening as I bumbled through another dry lesson about a missionary in a third-world country, I noticed that the group of girls before me could care less about what God was doing "over there." They were too busy trying to work their way through adolescent woes, such as where they fit in, how they could be popular, and how in the world they could get those boys to notice and like them. It occurred to me that we were not giving them any Biblical direction for what mattered the most to them at that point in their lives. *Déjà vu* hit me like a wrecking ball. The Holy Spirit laid an itchy wool blanket over my soul and said, "Former pit-dweller, you will now help these children avoid the land mines you so willingly walked through. I restored your mutilated body and lifted your shame-bowed head. Do everything in your power to keep these I entrust to you from walking the path that you walked."

I decided that I would find an age-appropriate Bible study dealing with the topic of purity, walk them through the simple steps to maintaining their purity, and feel so good about myself when it was over. Funny, that's not how my God works.

He spoke to me and said, "Oh no, child. You will research, toil, and write this yourself. You will examine what My word says and talk about how you diverged from it. You will know what My perfect path is and honestly present how hard it will be, how much it will cost, and how rewarding it will be to go against everything the world embraces to follow Me." In truth, I don't even remember writing it. I don't know where the words came from. I recall practically nothing of the entire process except the tears I cried and the anguish I felt at the sin I had buried and justified. When I resurfaced, I had a poorly—but passionately—compiled set of lessons on what

God's word has to say about the purity of a young person. Not only did the lessons include discussions on sex, but they also delved into the influence of the media, peer pressure, attitudes, busyness, appearance, drugs and alcohol, and forgiveness.

I presented it to my pastor and asked my Bible study group to pray. I waited to see if it would be worthy of sharing. When some legalistic—albeit well-meaning—church members questioned the teaching of such subject matter by a divorced and remarried woman, I bristled like a rabid dog. The doubt, shame, insecurity, and pride were sucking me into a vortex of self-pity. God, however, wouldn't let me abandon His will. He had forgiven me too much to let me whine my way into inaction. The pastor called me and asserted that we must proceed with the curriculum to shepherd these young girls. He reviewed the lessons and assured me that the Spirit had directed me to write a biblically sound study. Darn it, I thought I was off the hook on this one, but the Lord had other plans.

The difficult part comes each time I hold a parent meeting before I begin a session. I have to swallow the choking pride that tries to well up. God calls me to admit that my wretched past demands that I provide a life ring to their innocent daughters. I am compelled to tell them that they cannot ignore the subject—that not exposing them to God's naked truth will leave them victim to Satan's lies and traps. I am always astonished that instead of shunning me as the pariah, the Holy Spirit softens their hearts to see me as a redeemed daughter of the King.

These young women need to know the truth of 1 Timothy 4:12.

- Read this verse and list the ways in which everyone—but the young in particular—should be an example to the world.

The rewards have been heady beyond any earthly pleasure. The relationships I enjoy with the girls I have loved and prayed for are so sweet. I cried tears of thankfulness and triumph for Jesus the day the mother of one of the first girls I taught told me that her daughter had gone to her marriage bed a virgin.

It *can* happen in the twenty-first century. I'm sure Satan will bombard these handmaidens of Christ, but he better watch out—they are armed with an infallible sword. I make sure these precious girls are fully aware of 1 Peter 5:8–9.

- Write these verses from 1 Peter 5 in the space below.

91

As my own beautiful daughter graduates from high school this year and moves out to blaze her path through Satan's stomping grounds, I have a certain peace. I believe that I have broken a cycle of failure. I have sought to provide her with the sword of God's Word. It will equip her to discern the narrow path that God asks her to walk. She will stumble, and she may even fall. She may find herself at the bottom of a miry pit one day, but she will know that the only lover she needs to fulfill her completely is Jesus, the lover of her soul.

My fourth and final child is also a lovely girl. I pray that God will keep me mindful of the gravity of the responsibility of handing down a godly legacy that He entrusts to us as parents, women, and ransomed sinners. We must pass the weapons of truth, faith, and love to the next generation. It may expose the rawest of wounds, but the healing balm of Christ's blood will soothe the pain of a shameful past. The legacy of hope and redemption is worth whatever we must sacrifice to pass it on.

- Jeremiah 6:16 is one of Channy's life verses. Fill in the blanks from this verse: "This is what the Lord says, "Stand at the _____ and look; _____ for the ancient paths, ask where the _____ _____ is, and walk in it, and you will find _____ for your souls."

Channy's testimony of faithfulness to teach young women the benefits of living a holy life should remind each of us of the need to practice holiness in our own lives. As with all of us who are still breathing earth's air, Channy's legacy is still a work in process. However, the legacy left by her precious daddy, who died in 2006, was made especially sweet when he accepted Jesus as his Lord and Savior in the spring of 2005. Today he lives in heaven with Jesus, and one day Channy and her family will see him again.

MEDITATION MOMENT: God's specialty is making beauty from ashes, as we read in Channy's story. Spend some time journaling about a situation in your life where God has either already done this miraculous work or an area where you need for Him to do this work. Take time to acknowledge that He is able.

Day 3—Finally, I Know Him!

My legacy-building friend, I cannot tell you how excited I am about this day of our study. Throughout the writing of the study, I knew basically how I wanted every week of study to look—with the exception of this week. From the beginning, I prayed and prayed for the Lord to give me the perfect way to wrap up the study. I desired to finish well.

After several weeks of writing and praying, the Lord revealed to me what shape the final week would take. It would be comprised of a combination of legacy success stories and a personal time of introspection and evaluation. Great!

Then I realized that I still had to decide which legacy success stories to use. More prayer and seeking. As you have already seen, my own story was included, as well as that of my friend, Channy. Our stories were ones that dealt with our character and holiness as portions of our legacy. I realized that I needed a legacy success story dealing with faith. I thought, prayed, and talked to a few people, but nothing seemed to work out.

Then I remembered my friend Cynthia and the story of her journey to faith in Christ. Why didn't I think of her before? Her story is perfect. She has a story of a faith journey that should set even the most skeptical heart aflame. So without further ado, I offer you—in her own words—the faith journey of my dear friend, Dr. Cynthia Libert.

I know God. Finally, I know Him. He has known and loved me all along, and now I know and love Him on a deep, personal level. I am thirty-four years old and have been a seeker of God all my life. This is my story of how I found Him.

Although we were not a very religious family, my parents sent my sister and me to Saint Peter and Paul Catholic grade school in Collinsville, IL, hoping that we would develop a good moral framework. At school, I was taught the basics of the New Testament and attended mass on a weekly basis. I went through the motions of the sacraments—baptism as an infant, Holy Communion as a young child, and Confirmation at the age of thirteen. Our parents and teachers, however, did not encourage us to read the Bible. The religion I was taught seemed to be based on dogma, fear, and guilt.

During my adolescence, I went through a process of rebellion. I was analytical and skeptical. I discarded all of the dogma that I was taught as a child at the Catholic grade school. I went on to a public high school and then to St. Louis University—a Jesuit liberal arts college—where I continued my pursuit of truth. I had a strong intellectual curiosity and a voracious appetite for knowledge. I studied science, math, chemistry, physics, nature, history, art, literature, world religions, philosophy, psychology, feminism, and the like. I thought that if I studied enough, then one day I would gain wisdom and find God. I got glimpses of truth and beauty along the way, but there were so many questions—so many nagging, seemingly insurmountable questions that blocked my quest for faith.

As I studied at the college level, I was outraged to learn about the oppression of women throughout the ages and of all the violence in history. Religion seemed to be a device for power-hungry men to control people. My studies left me with a profound mistrust of authority and of our historical record. Consequently, I rejected the notion of faith in organized religion. In fact, I questioned if Jesus of Nazareth was even a historical person or merely a mythical figure. The existence of other major world religions and the differences within Christianity seemed to prove to me that no one can really know the truth. In short, I believed that Christianity was a human construct, and its claims to Truth were arrogant and irrational.

You see, Cynthia had bought Satan's lie.

- Read Colossians 2:8 and fill in the blanks: "See to it that no one takes you captive through _____ and deceptive philosophy, which depends on _____ _____ and the basic principles of this _____ rather than on Christ."

Additional personal and intellectual questions surfaced. I wondered why an all-loving, all-powerful God hadn't made Himself known to *me*. At the time, I felt that I was trying hard to know Him; yet there seemed to be no response from Him—just emptiness. I had a difficult time understanding the concept of faith. I wondered why others had it and I didn't. I believed that studying, reflecting, and trying to be a good person should be enough to satisfy God. I assumed that since God made me, He should know how I think and not make it so hard to get to the truth. I got hung up on the problem of explaining why God allows so much evil and suffering in the world. In my mind, organized religion was to blame for the violence and corruption perpetrated in the name of the Church. I thought that if there was a loving God, then

He would have compassion for me and put an end to my intellectual and spiritual turmoil. I wrestled with these questions for years.

What Cynthia did not understand was this principle from the mouth of the apostle Paul: "The man without the Spirit does not accept the things that come from the Spirit of God, for they are foolishness to him, and he cannot understand them, because they are spiritually discerned" (1 Corinthians 2:14).

- What or who is required in order for us to understand and accept the things of God?

- To a person without the Spirit of God residing in them, the things of God are considered to be what?

During college, I signed up for classes on topics such as Catholic morality and Human Sexuality, Evil, World Religions, Theology and Philosophy—but none of them gave me the answers for which I had been searching. I left college resigned to the belief that we cannot know the truth. My Christian education, however, did leave me with a sense of moral duty to lead an ethical life and to serve others. I followed my passion for science and my desire to help others and enrolled in a Jesuit medical school, Loyola University of Chicago. My seven years of medical school and residency training instilled in me a profound understanding and appreciation for the exquisite, miraculous nature of the human body and mind. This alone was enough to give me a strong belief that there is a creator. In addition to the wonders of our humanity, I also felt the presence of a creator to be self-evident in the natural world. The miracle of birth, butterflies, zebras, ecosystems, DNA, and the rise and setting of the sun were all awesome, but there were still many unanswered questions, especially regarding the existence of disease, suffering, and evil.

Surprisingly, despite attending a Jesuit college and medical school, I never read much of the Bible. I still held a strong mistrust of history and believed that the Bible was an odd collection of ancient stories pieced together to control people. Without a biblical worldview, I rejected the idea of human beings being born sinful. I did not believe in the devil, so it was difficult for me to reconcile the idea of an awesome Creator with the reality of our imperfect world. I studied the varied theological explanations for evil, but they did not satisfy me. In particular, I was haunted by the Grand Inquisitor character in Fyodor Dostoyevsky's famous novel, *The Brothers Karamazov.* He left me questioning and angry at a God who would design a universe that would include so much suffering as a necessary evil.

After medical school, I moved to Asheville, NC to complete my residency training in family medicine. By my late twenties, I was a wife and mother of a young daughter. My medical training was physically exhausting, spiritually depleting, and all-consuming. I looked for comfort and answers in Buddhism, Taoism, mysticism, and existentialism. I would occasionally attend services at a place called Jubilee that attempted to blend all the world religions into a harmonious whole. I tried to settle into an inclusive world view that acknowledges the wisdom of all religious traditions—a "One River, Many Wells" philosophy. For many reasons, this world view was not emotionally, intellectually, or spiritually satisfying, and I gave up hope of having a religious tradition. I wasn't even sure that I needed one, anyway. I convinced myself that I was at peace—or at least as satisfied as I thought was possible for a rational being. I fondly remembered the teachings of Jesus that I learned as a youth—and truth be told, I secretly wished that Jesus was real. However, there were just too many questions. Christianity was a large, jagged pill that I just couldn't swallow.

After my family medicine residency, I still hungered for a sense of community and connection with something larger than myself. I convinced my husband to attend the local Unitarian Universalist Fellowship (UUF) with me. I continued to view organized religion as suspect, but I wanted to give our daughter a moral framework like my parents did for me. I chose the UUF because it is a liberal, religious organization that promotes humanistic values and is not founded on any creed or dogma. Individual members may identify themselves as atheist, agnostic, Buddhist, humanist, pagan, or as ascribing to any other philosophical or religious traditions. This all-inclusive approach seemed to satisfy some of my philosophical objections to organized religion, but I still felt empty and found no peace.

My first job after residency was as a staff physician at a community health center in Hendersonville, NC. I was naïve and wanted to change the world. My ideals clashed with the harsh realities of modern medicine. I discovered that much of what we do as doctors is put band-aids over problems. We "sweep the problem under the drug." I had unrealistic hopes of somehow helping people heal their situations. I wanted to connect with my patients on a spiritual level, but at the time, I had no clue how to do so. I burned out in a short two years. I found myself struggling with anxiety, depressed moods, and physical symptoms related to stress. How ironic! I should have been on top of the world. I was a young, healthy physician with a loving husband, precious baby daughter, beautiful home, and a new career in medicine. I thought I could fix my mood if I found a solution to the problems I was facing in my medical career. I spent over a year designing my ideal practice using holistic medicine approaches in a spa-like setting. I even hired consultants and talked to bankers about financing. The whole thing was overwhelming. I was lost.

In December of 2006, I got an unexpected phone call from my good friend and fellow family physician, Michele Thompson. She wanted to know if I would move to Blairsville and start a medical practice with her. I had never even traveled to the mountains of North Georgia, but I was at a fork in the road—my very own hinge moment. I knew that I did not want to stay at my current job, and I had very recently decided to scrap my business plans. My husband and I took a leap of faith, jumped on the opportunity, and moved to Blairsville. We had no idea how it would turn out. I was concerned about moving deeper into the Bible Belt and wondered if the local people would accept me due to my status as a Yankee and a heathen.

In December 2007, Michele and her husband Stephen, both of whom are devout Christians, invited us to their home to exchange Christmas gifts. I engaged the two of them in a conversation about their faith. I remember at the end of our conversation thinking that I had not heard anything new. My low opinion of Christianity was about the same. I had a vague sense of envy about the peace and certainty they had as a result of their Christian faith, but I continued to feel superior intellectually, since I felt no need to submit to such a belief system in order to cope with the suffering and uncertainty of life. I felt mature and worldly.

My closing comment that evening to Stephen and Michele was something to the effect of, "I am a good person. I feel that I have earnestly pursued God over the course of my life. Why do I not have faith?"

Stephen's answer still resides in my heart: "I don't know, Cindy, but I do know because of your background and who you are, you have the potential to be a really great Christian someday."

I was amused. We both smiled and laughed, and I left the party thinking, "How arrogant and predictable! It is so typical that he would respond that way!" Little did I know the cosmic joke was on me!

A week later, I attended a Christmas concert at the First Baptist Church in Blairsville in which Stephen was performing. At the end of the performance, the pastor, Dr. Fred Lodge, asked us to take a moment to ask Jesus to come into our lives. I was moved to do so with an open and hopeful heart. My life has not been the same. The change was not instantaneous. There were no angels or a beam of light coming down from Heaven. Yet at that moment, I was no longer angry with God for being absent from my life. I realized that this was the first time that I earnestly repented of my sins and asked Jesus to live through me.

The year after I accepted Christ as my Savior was rocky. I had lots of doubts, psychological pains, and emotional struggles, but I persisted in prayer and kept asking God to reveal himself to me in truth. I read the Bible frequently and started to piece together the history of God's people, the Jews, and the beautiful connection between the Old and New Testament. I read numerous other books, such as *The Purpose-Driven Life, The Case for Christ*, and *Classic Christianity,* to name just a few. Old ideas fell away, and my worldview shifted. I got involved with a ministry called Mothers of Preschoolers. I enrolled my children in Sunday school, Mission Friends, choir, and Vacation Bible School. I attended church regularly and listened to praise and worship music. In short, I immersed myself in the body of Christ.

The following has emerged as my life verse: "Do not conform any longer to the pattern of this world, but be transformed by the renewing of your mind. Then you will be able to test and approve what God's will is—his good, pleasing and perfect will" (Romans 12:2).

I am now painfully and acutely aware of the rebellion that kept me from walking with the Lord sooner—namely arrogance, elitism, foolishness, pessimism, pride, and fear. My heart was hard and skeptical from years of academia and the influence of worldly principles. I thought that I had to figure out all the answers for myself! I now know the truth in God's promise from Luke 11:9–10.

- Fill in the blanks from this verse: "So I say to you: _____ and it will be given to you; _____ and you will find; _____ and the door will be opened to you. For everyone who asks receives; he who seeks finds; and to him who knocks, the door will be opened."

Matthew 11:26–30 also became key verses for Cynthia. In it, Jesus urges us, "Come to me, all you who are weary and burdened, and I will give you rest. Take my yoke upon you and learn from me, for I am gentle and humble in heart, and you will find rest for your souls. For my yoke is easy and my burden is light."

I was born again as a Christian the December evening when I prayed with Dr. Lodge and asked Jesus into my heart. From that moment on, my life has been progressively transformed through my relationship with Jesus Christ. On March 29, 2009, during a celebration of the Passover at the First Baptist Church, I encountered God's Holy Spirit in what I can only describe as one of my peak life experiences. I did not anticipate it. Words fail me when I attempt to describe it. In the months prior, I had been studying the Old Testament and the Passover story. As we went through the process of breaking the bread and drinking the juice, I understood God speaking to me through the body and blood of Jesus Christ. An indescribable sense of cleansing washed over me. I was freed from the nagging doubts that separated me from the peace of Christ. I felt a sense of community and connection that I had previously never experienced. I was at home. The following week, I publicly professed Jesus Christ as my Savior, and on May 24, 2009, I was baptized.

Before I became a Christian, I was hurting, exhausted, angry, resentful, and tense. I saw Christianity as a weakness. It seemed to be the opposite of self-reliance and the American way. By the world's standards, I had accomplished a lot for a woman of thirty years of age. Yet I had spent my life battling perfectionism, and was under immense, self-imposed pressure to succeed. I defined my self-worth by attempting to measure up to the unobtainable ideal in my own mind. I thought that I had to "worry my way to success" through sheer willpower and hard work. What an oppressive way to live! Now it is with great joy and peace that I embrace God's command: "Do not be anxious about anything, but in everything, by prayer and petition, with thanksgiving, present your requests to God. And the peace of God, which transcends all understanding, will guard your hearts and your minds in Christ Jesus" (Philippians 4:6–7).

A short time ago, I was unable to fathom the concept of faith. Now I cherish my faith as one of the most precious gifts in my life. The study of God's Word and spending time in prayer enable me to experience deeper, more meaningful and fruitful relationships with my husband, children, friends, and family, as well as with the Lord. My practice as a doctor has been transformed. I used to struggle daily with feelings of resentment about the demands of my work. Now I know that God has called me to do my work, and it brings me great peace, joy, and fulfillment. I feel privileged to do the work that I do, and I enjoy the great responsibility that God has given me to minister to my patients.

I rest in the confidence of my salvation. God loves me and is with me always. I have no doubt that there will be continued suffering and more questions to face in life; yet it is wonderful to have God's Word in my heart. On a daily basis, God gives me the answers and reassurance I need to address all of my questions and troubles. One of the greatest testaments to the power of God in my life has been the complete healing of my anxiety and depressive symptoms. Despite the ongoing trials in my life, these emotions do not have a hold on me any longer. I trust that God will work out all things for my good and for His glory.

As I look back over my life, it is with both awe and complete confidence that I know God has been with me every step of the way. I rejoice to finally have the awareness that God is my constant companion. It gives me meaning, purpose, joy, peace, and fulfillment. I am a living testimony of how God can completely transform your life through Jesus Christ. What a precious legacy of spiritual wisdom to pass on to my children! I know that together with my husband Pete, I am giving our daughters, Leah and Ana, a firm foundation on which to build their faith. Instead of letting the world teach our children that they need to "find themselves" in this complex, harsh, dog-eat-dog world, we can share the good news that we find our true meaning, purpose, and identity in Christ! When they experience the inevitable trials of life, we can encourage them to find the perfect comfort, strength, and peace in the living Word of God. During their earthly lives, it is my prayer that they discover and fully explore the enduring joy, hope, and confidence that is gained by a daily walk with God. Above all else, I pray that they experience the eternal, beautiful, and precious gift of a relationship with our living, risen Lord, Jesus Christ!

Every time I read Dr. Cynthia's testimony, I am left speechless. Her story tells of an honest seeker who looked at all the options and made the decision for Jesus. She has never regretted her decision. I wish you could sit and visit with her like I am privileged to do on a regular basis. Every time I am with her, my faith is challenged and enriched by her excitement about Jesus and what He has done in her life. I hope that you were touched by her story as well. Your faith is the crucial cornerstone for a godly legacy, and being able to tell your story about how Jesus has changed your life is so important.

MEDITATION MOMENT: Today, I am asking you to take the time and write out your story of faith. When did you come to faith in Jesus? How old were you? What was your life like before you met Jesus? Where were you? Who was instrumental in your discovery of Jesus as the boss of your life? What difference has knowing Him made in your life? Include any and all pertinent details about your journey to faith.

Day 4—A Legacy Check-Up

I think as we grow older, we go to the doctor or dentist for annual check-ups with at least the slightest bit of apprehension. What will they find? Have I gained too much weight? I wonder if that mole is anything to be worried about. Is my blood pressure too high? My mother had high cholesterol. Will mine be high, too? Will I have any cavities? Then, after we see the doctor or the dentist, we don't even get any sort of fun prize for being a big girl and not crying when they tortured us by pricking our finger with one of those sticky-pokey things! Good grief, it just isn't right!

When you visit your doctor or dentist for your annual check-up, she has a list of areas that need to be examined in order to assure your physical health. In addition, if they draw blood or take other samples from your body, there are normal values against which your results are compared. In short, there is a standard of care that your doctor uses to evaluate your health.

For our final two days, we are headed into God's exam room for a check-up—a legacy check-up. Quite possibly, today and tomorrow could be the hardest days of work that we have done in these six weeks. Ah, but it is even more possible that these days could be the most rewarding of this study. So let's get to it. The sooner we get started, the sooner we get moving toward a godly legacy.

First, I want to remind you of the areas of your legacy that we will be checking—namely your faith, character, and holiness. Second, I will give you references—or normal values, as we in medicine like to call them. You will look up these references in your Bible, write them out, and compare your personal results with what Scripture says they should be. Finally, you will do a personal evaluation on what you find when you do this comparison. You will grade your legacy using the following scale:

- Excellent

- Needs some work

- Not even close

- Better get started

I hope that you will find that you rarely or never answer "better get started"—but if you do, please know that this is your opportunity to begin working in earnest on your legacy. Today we will perform a check-up on our faith. Tomorrow we will finish up with our character and our holiness.

Please do not rush through these exercises, because they are crucial if you desire to honestly assess where you are on the legacy-building scale.

I am asking you—in fact, I am begging you—to stop right now and pray. Ask the Lord to help you honestly take inventory of the issues surrounding your legacy. He desires for you to leave a godly legacy, and He stands ready to reveal the things to you that need some work. Ask Him to show you anything and everything that would help you have a clear picture of where you currently are in this matter of your legacy. There is so much as stake here. Please be honest with yourself and with God.

Legacy and Faith Check-up

1. Legacy Consideration—Prior to doing this study, had you ever thoughtfully considered what you want the generations that come behind you to remember about you?

    a.   Normal reference: Proverbs 5:21 (write out the verse completely)

    b.   Personal Evaluation: Excellent   Better Get Started

2. Salvation—In Week 1, Day 5, we delved into the plan that God put in place for our salvation. Is there a time in your past when you recognized your need for Jesus to be the boss, the king, and the ruler of your life? Did you ask Him to come into your heart and live with you forever?

    a.   Normal Reference: Romans 10:9 (write out the verse completely)

    b.   Personal Evaluation: Excellent   Better Get Started

3. Faith—Max Lucado said that faith is "the conviction that He [God] can and the hope that He will." Overall, how would you rate your faith? Do you believe that God is who He says He is and that He will keep His promises to you?

    a.   Normal Reference: Hebrews 11:1–2 (write out the verses completely)

    b.   Personal Evaluation: Excellent   Needs Some Work

                                     Not Even Close   Better Get Started

4. Faith in Action—When God asks you to do something, are you obedient? It has been said that partial obedience is disobedience. How would you rate your obedience to God?

    a.   Normal Reference: Hebrews 11:8 (write out the verse completely)

b.   Personal Evaluation: Excellent   Needs Some Work

                                                       Not Even Close   Better Get Started

5.   God's Faithful Presence—God has promised to never forsake us—to never leave us once we are His child through the blood of Jesus Christ. Deep in the marrow of your bones, do you really believe that God will never forsake you?

      a.   Normal Reference: Deuteronomy 31:8 (write out the verse completely)

      b.   Personal Evaluation: Excellent   Needs Some Work

                                                        Not Even Close   Better Get Started

6.   Faith in Trials—It is easy to have faith in God when our lives are rolling along smoothly. The true test of our faith is when trials and troubles strike. When trials come, do you cling tightly to God and trust Him to walk with you, or do you struggle to fix things on your own? How does your faith look in the middle of trials?

      a.   Normal Reference: Isaiah 43:1–3a (write out the verses completely)

      b.   Personal Evaluation: Excellent   Needs Some Work

                                                        Not Even Close   Better Get Started

I am going to ask you to do something out of the ordinary with today's material. If at all possible, within the next twelve hours, please take some time to review your answers from your work today. Once again, ask the Lord to reveal any hidden information that needs to be brought into the light in this matter of your legacy. Ask Him to show you if any of your answers were not well thought-out and completely honest. Be willing to re-think anything that He sheds insight on that might need changing. Then make the following prayer your own by personalizing it to your life situation.

"Lord, I come to You this day in complete humility, seeking to do whatever is necessary to assure that I leave a godly legacy for the generations that come behind me. I thank You that a godly legacy is what You desire for me, and I acknowledge that You stand ready to help me make the changes that are necessary to leave that godly legacy. I ask You to keep this legacy front and center in my mind as I go throughout my days, because I understand that it is the collection of seconds, minutes, hours, and days that make up my legacy.

"Father, please show me where my faith needs to grow. Help me to step out in obedience the moment I sense You calling me to follow You. Forgive me for the times that I hesitate or procrastinate. Help me to believe that no matter what You allow me to go through, You are walking beside me, before me, and behind me; guiding, protecting, and covering me. I am Your dearly loved child. Help me to hold tightly to that knowledge in good times and in bad so that others can see in me a faith in You that makes them desire a closer walk with You. I desire a treasure chest legacy, Lord. Thank you for helping me to create that. Amen."

Day 5—Legacy Check-up: Part Two

In season four of the political thriller *24,* agent Jack Bauer is attempting to stop a terrorist from blowing up Air Force One, on which the president of the United States is traveling. The terrorist is a former American military pilot who holds a huge grudge against America. He was a highly decorated warrior during his years of service in the military, and Jack hopes to remind him of those years as he seeks to dissuade the pilot from launching the missile that will blow up Air Force One. Bauer is communicating with the terrorist via a telephone connection.

Jack tells the terrorist, whose name is Anderson, that he knows about Anderson's extremely successful military career and how his bravery led to numerous medals and honors.

Agent Bauer then says, "Captain Anderson, what you are trying to do right now—that's not who you are. That is not how you want to be remembered."

Jack understood the concept of legacy, and he was trying to get Captain Anderson to do a quick legacy check-up in order to avert disaster.

Is the way that you are living right now how you want to be remembered?

Let's continue our legacy check-up today as we close our time together examining the legacy that we are leaving for the generations that come behind us. Today we will check up on our character and our holiness. Today's work will likely be more difficult than yesterday's, so please stop right now and pray, asking the Lord to help you honestly search your heart with regard to your character and your holiness. Ask Him to show you *any* area that needs the work of the Holy Spirit applied to it in order to conform to the image of Christ.

- Take a moment and look up Romans 12:1–2 and write it below. Turn it into a prayer as you ask the Lord to help you create your own legacy.

After you have prayed, please complete the following, being totally honest and transparent with yourself and with God. We will use the same format that we used yesterday.

Character and Holiness Check-up

1. The fruit of the Spirit as detailed in Galatians 5 is an excellent plumb line for assessing your character. How does your life measure up to the fruit of the Spirit? Are you exhibiting these fruits on a regular basis?

a.	Normal Reference: Galatians 5:22–23 (write out the verse completely)

b.	Personal Evaluation:	Excellent		Needs Some Work

			Not Even Close		Better Get Started

2.	Gossip is a huge issue as we think about our character. So often we pass along gossip and do not even realize that we are doing it. This habit has become so much a part of our normal conversation that we are oblivious to its potential damage in other people's lives. Do you pass along information about other people without being asked to do so by the parties involved? Do you get personal satisfaction out of being in the know and able to let others know what you know?

a.	Normal Reference: Titus 2:3 (write out the verse completely)

b.	Personal Evaluation:	Excellent		Needs Some Work

			Not Even Close		Better Get Started

3.	Our culture today views lying as sometimes being necessary. God says that a lying tongue is something that He despises. How do you score on this issue? Do you tell the truth in love—*always?*

a.	Normal Reference: Proverbs 12:22 (write out the verse completely)

b.	Personal Evaluation:	Excellent		Needs Some Work

			Not Even Close		Better Get Started

4.	It was not too many decades ago that much business was conducted on a handshake and a promise. Men and women could be counted on to keep their word. If a person made a promise, they could be trusted to do what they promised. This is not so today in many circles. Can those who interact with you have complete confidence in you? Are you trustworthy and loyal, even if going back on your word would seem to benefit you? If you make a promise, do you keep it?

    a.   Normal Reference: 2 Corinthians 7:16 (write out the verse completely)

    b.   Personal Evaluation: Excellent   Needs Some Work

                                                  Not Even Close   Better Get Started

5.   God commands us to be holy. This is not a suggestion, but a command. To be holy means to be set apart, to be pure, honorable, and yes, even godlike. Walking in holiness means making some difficult and perhaps unpopular decisions. Do you seek to live a holy life before God?

    a.   Normal Reference: Leviticus 11:44a (write out the verse completely)

    b.   Personal Evaluation: Excellent   Needs Some Work

                                                  Not Even Close   Better Get Started

6.   Modest dressing seems to be out of style in our day. In truth, modesty never goes out of style. Do you seek to dress in a stylish, yet modest fashion? Do your tops and blouses fit well without showing cleavage or being too tight? Are your skirts and shorts an appropriate length? Do you dress with dignity and in a way that honors yourself and the Lord?

    a.   Normal Reference: Proverbs 31:25a (write out the verse completely)

    b.   Personal Evaluation: Excellent   Needs Some Work

                                                  Not Even Close   Better Get Started

7.   Sexual sin wreaks havoc on the body and mind. God will not allow one of His children to live in sin without significant consequences. Are you engaged in sexual sin? Pre-marital sex? Extra-marital affairs? Pornography? Flirting with a married man? There will be consequences for this type of sin, and they will not be good. How do you measure up to God's standard for sexual purity?

a.   Normal Reference: 1 Thessalonians 4:3–5 (write out the verse completely)

b.   Personal Evaluation: Excellent   Needs Some Work

Not Even Close   Better Get Started

8. On Day 5 of Week 5, we talked about shunning the appearance of evil, and we listed several scenarios where this advice might be put into practice. Are you careful to never put yourself in situations where your holiness might be compromised such as those listed in that day of study? This question would be easy to gloss over. I beg you to seriously consider your answer to this question, my friend.

a.   Normal Reference: Proverbs 10:9 (write out the verse completely)

b.   Personal Evaluation: Excellent   Needs Some Work

Not Even Close   Better Get Started

The end of a Bible study is a bittersweet time for me. It has been my privilege and my absolute joy to take this journey toward a godly legacy with you. Now we must go our separate ways and put into practice what the Lord has taught us in our time together. Although you and I will part here, Jesus will go on with you. His Holy Spirit will enable you to live a life that leaves a godly legacy for the generations that come behind you if you will allow Him.

Will you always get it right? Probably not. Neither will I. But that does not mean we stop trying. We need to be intentional about leaving godly legacies for the generations that come behind us. You cannot build my legacy, and I cannot build yours. We are each responsible for our own legacies. So I will leave you with this challenge:

1. Every day, at the beginning of the day, take time to purpose in your heart that with God's help, you will make godly choices that day.

2. Regularly take time to examine the lives of people who have left great legacies and make a decision to imitate their choices as much as possible.

3. Stay diligent in your prayer life and time spent in God's Word.

4. Remember that your character is more important than your reputation.

5. Finally, ask God to help you increase your holiness each day.

Perhaps one day you and I will have a chance to sit over a cup of coffee or a glass of sweet iced tea and chat about how this study has impacted your legacy building efforts—if not here on earth, then most assuredly in heaven. So until that time arrives, be mindful of your legacy and what you are leaving for the generations that come behind you. I'm praying for you, my friend.

Bibliography

1. Encarta Dictionary.

2. Wiersbe, Warren (1993). *Be Strong: Putting God's Power to Work in Your Life.* Colorado Springs, Colorado:David C Cook. P. 42

3. Swindoll, C. W. (1998). *Swindoll's Ultimate Book of Illustrations & Quotes.* Nashville: Thomas Nelson . p. 193-194.

4. Zodhiates, Spiros (1996). *Hebrew-Greek Key Word Study Bible.* Chattanooga, Tennessee: AMG Publishers. p. 1662.

5. *Life Application Bible: New International Version.* Wheaton, Illinois: Tyndale House Publishers and Grand Rapids, Michigan: Zondervan Publishing House. Study notes p. 2236.

6. Peterson, Eugene H. (2003). *The Message Remix: The Bible in Contemporary Language.* Colorado Springs, Colorado: Navpress.

7. Hall, Ron and Moore, Denver (2006). *Same Kind of Different As Me.* Nashville, Tennessee: Thomas Nelson Publishers. P. 103

8. Naked Eyes Album *Burning Bridges.* 1983.

9. Life Application Bible: New International Version. Study notes p. 2236.

10. Peterson, Eugene H. (2003). *The Message Remix: The Bible in Contemporary Language.*

11. Strobel, Lee (1998). *The Case for Christ: A Journalist's Personal Investigation of the Evidence for Jesus Christ.* Grand Rapids, Michigan:Zondervan. p.177

12. Rowell, Edward K and Leadership (2008). *1001 Quotes, Illustrations, and Humorous Stories for Preachers, Teachers, and Writers.* Grand Rapids, Michigan: Baker Books. P. 141

13. Noonan, Peggy (2001). *When Character Was King: A Story of Ronald Reagan.* New York, New York: Viking. P. 254

14. Encarta Dictionary

15. Zodhiates, Spiros (1996). *Hebrew-Greek Key Word Study Bible*. Chattanooga, Tennessee: AMG Publishers.

16. Ibid.

17. Cooper, David C (2007). *Timeless Truths in Changing Times*. Cleveland, Tennessee: Pathway Press. P. 219.

18. Peterson, Eugene H. (2003). *The Message Remix: The Bible in Contemporary Language.*

19. Hee Haw Transcripts online.

20. Rowell, Edward K and Leadership (2008). *1001 Quotes, Illustrations and Humorous Stories for Preachers, Teachers, and Writers.* P. 314

21. Swindoll, Charles (1997). *Esther: A Woman of Strength and Dignity*. Nashville, Tennessee: W Publishing Group.

22. A Study of Values and Behavior Concerning Integrity: The Impact of Age, Cycicism and High School Character. A Report of The Josephson Institute of Ethics. 2009

23. Journal of Moral Education. Volume. 38, Issue 3. September 2009

24. Lucado, Max. *Just Like Jesus*. 2003.

25. Ashcroft, John (1998). *Lessons From A Father To His Son*. Nashville, Tennessee: Thomas Nelson Publishers. pp 40.41

26. *The New Strong's Expanded Exhaustive Concordance of the Bible- Hebrew and Aramaic Dictionary.* 2001

27. Ibid

28. Personal Communication

29. Zodhiates, Spiros (1996). *Hebrew-Greek Key Word Study Bible.*

30. Bridges, Jerry (1978). *The Pursuit of Holiness*. Colorado Springs, Colorado: NavPress. P.32

31. Peterson, Eugene H. (2003). *The Message Remix: The Bible in Contemporary Language.*

32. Feldhahn, Shaunti (2004). *For Women Only: What You Need to Know About the Inner Lives of Men*. Colorado Springs, Colorado: Multnomah Publishers.

33. Ibid.

34. Ibid.

35. Ibid.

36. The Point blog.

37. Peterson, Eugene H. (2003). *The Message Remix: The Bible in Contemporary Language.*

38. Zodhiates, Spiros (1996). *Hebrew-Greek Key Word Study Bible.*

39. Bridges, Jerry (1978). *The Pursuit of Holiness*. P.84

CPSIA information can be obtained at www.ICGtesting.com
Printed in the USA
LVOW02s0732140713

342769LV00001B/21/P

9 781615 073337